the student cookbook

the student
cookbook

hamlyn

First published in Great Britain in 2004 by
Hamlyn, a division of Octopus Publishing Group Ltd,
2–4 Heron Quays, London E14 4JP

Copyright © Octopus Publishing Group Ltd 2004

ISBN-13: 978-0-600-60965-0
ISBN-10: 0-600-60965-0

A CIP catalogue record for this book is available
from the British Library

Printed and bound in China

10 9 8 7 6

Notes

This books includes dishes made with nuts and nut
derivatives. It is advisable for those with known
allergic reactions to nuts and nut derivatives and
those who may be potentially vulnerable to these
allergies, such as pregnant and nursing mothers,
invalids, the elderly, babies and children, to avoid
dishes made with nuts and nut oils. It is also prudent
to check the labels of preprepared ingredients for the
possible inclusion of nut derivatives.

The Department of Health advises that eggs should
not be consumed raw. This book contains some
dishes made with raw or lightly cooked eggs.
It is prudent for more vulnerable people such as
pregnant and nursing mothers, invalids, the elderly,
babies and young children to avoid uncooked or
lightly cooked dishes made with eggs.

Meat and poultry should be cooked thoroughly.
To test if poultry is cooked, pierce the flesh through
the thickest part with a skewer or fork – the juices
should run clear, never pink or red.

Both metric and imperial measurements are given
for the recipes. Use one set of measures only, not a
mixture of both.

Ovens should be preheated to the specified
temperature. If using a fan-assisted oven, follow the
manufacturer's instructions for adjusting the time
and temperature. Grills should also be preheated.

Contents

introduction

Your clothes and CDs are packed, you've said goodbye to your mates and you're looking forward to three years of late nights, undisturbed lie-ins and no nagging about cleaning your room or doing the washing up! Nothing quite beats the excitement of your first few weeks at college or university and, with cheap lager at the Student Union, freshers' week, and working out where you're supposed to be and when, the last thing on your mind is going to be cooking. However, once you've settled into the routine, you'll probably want to start making at least some attempt at using the kitchen, and this book will help to make that prospect a little less daunting. In fact, follow the advice here and try some of the recipes in this book and you never know, you might even begin to enjoy it!

Where's the kitchen?

As this is probably your first time living away from home, you may not be used to the complex workings of the kitchen and find the whole idea of shopping for, preparing and cooking a meal more frightening than going to the dentist. Sure, you've made the odd bacon sandwich, you probably know the difference between the microwave and the oven and you could even hazard a guess at the main ingredients for a trifle, but the mere thought of attempting a Sunday roast or inviting friends round for a lasagne makes you break out in a cold sweat. However, with just a little know-how, a few basic ingredients and some confidence (justified or otherwise!) you can turn mealtimes into a social occasion to rival happy hour at the local pub.

Once you've mastered the basics, and have progressed from scraping the burnt bits off toast for breakfast to preparing perfect poached eggs, the great enigma that is cooking will start to disappear and you'll wonder what all the fuss was about. After all, this isn't rocket science – it's just acquired instinct. It's about learning a recipe then having the confidence to adapt it, depending on what's in your fridge or cupboard. It's about experimenting with ingredients, trying out cooking techniques and creating a finished dish that you're proud of – whether it's a fancy shepherd's pie or an apple and blueberry smoothie, chunky choc cookies or a Mai Tai.

On a budget

You'll be on a tight budget and may well be loathe to donate too much beer money to the culinary cause, but with a little planning and some creative shopping you can eat really well on a small amount of money. An easy way to save your cash is to look out for special offers at the supermarket. You'll often see two-for-one deals and these can be great for stocking up on items you're going to be using a lot. However, don't get too carried away or you may end up grabbing ten packs of Peking Duck from the chiller cabinet only for it to sit in the fridge going off because you haven't got round to eating it all.

✱ tip

Try and stick to frozen goods (or items that you can freeze), tins and packets. You'll often get bargains on things like salad, bread and other perishable foods if you go towards the end of the day, but again, don't get carried away! Another tip is that when you're cooking, make double the amount, then freeze half – it's often not much more expensive to make a bit more, and then you have an extra meal.

Perfect partners

Bonnie and Clyde, Butch Cassidy and the Sundance Kid, Posh and Becks; as in life, great partnerships also exist in the kitchen, and there are certain ingredients that you can put together and know that they're going to taste great. You may have burnt the broccoli, forgotten to add the mince to the Bolognese sauce, or left the giblets in their plastic packaging inside the roast chicken, but fear not, include these combinations in your meals and disaster will be averted!

salt + pepper

These much-loved condiments are the saviour of many a bland sauce. Use sparingly, seasoning as you cook, and they will lift the flavours of everything from pasta sauces to scrambled eggs.

olive oil + balsamic vinegar

These two love each other – so much so, that if you place some of each in a screw-top jar and shake to combine, you have the perfect salad dressing. They'll quite happily be joined by a teaspoon of mustard, a drizzle of honey and a squeeze of lemon juice and, in fact, this combination also makes the ideal marinade for chicken.

chilli + garlic

These two are essential ingredients in many a tasty pasta sauce, stir-fry or curry. If you're a real fan you can always fry some extra and sprinkle it on top!

tomato + basil

Another classic culinary match made in heaven. Whether you use these two as the basis for a pasta sauce or serve a simple tomato salad garnished with basil leaves, they will ensure your meal is remembered.

Other great foodie partners include:
spinach + ricotta
peas + prawns
lamb + mint
onion + garlic
salmon + dill

In fact, that's really what good cooking is all about; finding flavours and ingredients that complement each other. That way, you can keep things simple – why make life complicated with long lists of ingredients to peel, wash and chop, when more often than not, less is more. So, on that note, let's look at how you can get away with the bare minimum of utensils and gadgets and still prepare a meal that will make your mother proud!

back to basics

Moving into a hall of residence or a shared house means you probably won't have the most luxurious or well-equipped kitchen in the world, but as long as it has four walls and a working oven, there's hope. As the old saying goes, 'A bad workman always blames his tools', and the fact is that you can prepare anything from a quick sandwich to a gourmet meal with just a few essential pieces of equipment and a well-stocked cupboard. Arrive with the following and you'll be set up for the year!

✱ Set of saucepans
These are absolutely essential if you're planning on doing any cooking at all. Buy three if possible – small, medium and large – as this will enable you to cook different ingredients at the same time. A large frying pan with a lid is also great for one-pot meals and means you don't necessarily have to invest in a casserole dish as well.

✱ Set of knives
Again, very important. Try and buy a couple of different sizes, as you'll need one for slicing bread, another for large vegetables and one for onions, garlic and other smaller vegetables. Make sure they are sharp.

✱ Chopping boards
It's a good idea to have two chopping boards – one for vegetables and bread, and one for chopping meat (plastic boards are best for this).

✱ Wok
Not essential but extremely useful. Stir-fries are cheap, healthy, easy and really quick to prepare in a wok.

✱ Set of utensils
You can buy these in a pack in many shops – make sure it includes a wooden spoon, spatula, ladle and potato masher. You'll also need a can opener, peeler and grater.

✱ Mixing bowl
Great for whisking eggs, making sauces and marinating meat in.

✱ Ovenproof dish
Very handy if you want to make any kind of pie, lasagne or roast. A baking tin will also come in handy.

✱ Colander
A very versatile piece of equipment. Not only will it ensure that your rice and pasta aren't waterlogged when you serve them, but it also doubles as a steamer if you buy a metal one.

Storecupboard essentials

Some ingredients crop up again and again in recipes so it's worth stocking up on them. That way, if you fancy a snack or quick dinner, you'll only need to buy a few extra things.

☐ **Salt and pepper** (freshly ground black pepper is best)
☐ **Good-quality olive oil** (for dressings, marinades and grilling)
☐ **Vegetable oil** (for frying and roasting)
☐ **Balsamic vinegar**
☐ **Soy sauce** (essential for stir-fries and for adding a salty flavour to dressings and marinades)
☐ **Butter or margarine**
☐ **Eggs**
☐ **Milk**
☐ **Onions**
☐ **Garlic**
☐ **Rice**
☐ **Couscous**
☐ **Pasta**
☐ **Potatoes**
☐ **Flour**
☐ **Dried spices** (curry powder, ground coriander, ground cumin, paprika and turmeric are used a lot)
☐ **Dried mixed herbs**
☐ **Mustard**
☐ **Cans of chopped tomatoes**
☐ **Tomato purée**

Balancing act

The stereotypical image of students living off baked beans, cheap bread and tuna pasta is very outdated. Just because you're going to university, it doesn't mean you're going to survive on carbohydrates alone, and count the orange part of a vodka and orange as your vitamin C intake. Although it's not always possible to get a balanced diet, as long as you make an effort to eat healthily, then the odd fry-up or takeaway won't be a problem.

The one easy rule to follow is to try to eat five portions of fruit and vegetables every day. This may sound impossible, especially when you take into account days lost to hangovers, but drink a glass of fruit juice or a smoothie with breakfast, have a piece of fruit with lunch and a salad with dinner and you're almost there. Steaming your vegetables instead of boiling them helps to retain most of the nutrients. You can use a colander for this – just bring a small amount of water to the boil in a saucepan and place the colander over the top with the vegetables in it.

There are simple changes that you can make in order to eat a more balanced diet, and moderation is the key. Cut down on snacks such as biscuits, cakes, crisps, sweets, chocolate, pies and fizzy drinks as they contain loads of sugar or fat. Plus they will give you short-term energy bursts, but then often leave you craving more as your blood sugar dips. You don't have to drop them completely from your diet, but try having some fruit, nuts, a yogurt or flapjack occasionally instead.

You also need to keep an eye on how much saturated fat you are eating (it's very easy for it to add up after a couple of late-night take-aways!), so use olive oil instead of butter for cooking and eat low-fat margarine or spreads instead of butter.

Your diet is likely to be based round carbohydrates, which are cheap and easy to cook. And although bread, cereals and potatoes are a great source of fibre, calcium, iron and B vitamins, instead of eating processed white bread, pasta and rice, choose wholegrain or wholemeal breads and cereals, which haven't had the vital nutrients refined out of them.

If you're a vegetarian, or just don't eat much meat, then it is important that you still get the B vitamins, iron, protein and zinc that meat is rich in. Eat foods such as beans, pulses, eggs and nuts. Tofu is also a great source of protein and calcium.

Fish is excellent brain food and it is recommended that you eat at least two portions of fresh fish a week. Cod, plaice and other white fish are relatively inexpensive and can be ready in under ten minutes. Just drizzle a little oil over the fish fillet and grill until cooked. Serve with a squeeze of lemon juice and broccoli and potatoes and you've got a delicious, healthy meal in no time at all.

Kitchen hygiene

Giving someone food poisoning isn't the best way to make friends when you start college, so you'll need to follow a few basic rules when you're cooking.

∗Always wash your hands in hot, soapy water before you start cooking and then again after handling any uncooked meat.

∗When storing meat and fish in the fridge, cover it well and always keep it on the lowest shelf, so juices don't drip onto other food.

∗When preparing uncooked meat, use a separate chopping board and knife and wash these well before using them again for other food.

∗Make sure you cook all meat properly. If it's cooked, the juices will run clear (not pink), when pierced through the thickest part of the meat with a skewer or fork.

∗Wash salad, fruit and vegetables thoroughly before using.

∗If you're reheating food, only do this once and make sure it's piping hot all the way through.

∗Use really hot water when washing-up – the hotter the water, the better it will be at killing germs.

Basic preparation

Here are just a few tips to get you started and help you gain a bit of confidence in the kitchen. Of course the best way to get the hang of preparing ingredients and food is through practice!

Before you begin

*Don't forget to take meat, chicken or fish out of the freezer to allow them to defrost thoroughly before cooking. Keep them in the fridge until ready to cook.

*Before you start cooking, make sure you have all the ingredients you need. This may sound obvious, but there's nothing worse than being halfway through a recipe and suddenly realising that someone has helped themselves to the vital ingredient.

*It's a good idea to do all the peeling, measuring, chopping etc. before you start. Put each ingredient in a bowl or on a plate, then you can cook without interruption.

*If you're cooking in the oven, make sure you preheat it to the correct temperature before you put the food in.

Rinsing

*Rinse rice thoroughly before cooking to get rid of the starch. This will stop the rice sticking together once cooked and it will also cook more quickly.

*When cooking potatoes, again rinse them well. Put in a pan of cold water as you're chopping them, then rinse and change the water before cooking.

Chopping

*When chopping an onion, peel it then rinse under cold, running water first. This should help to stop your eyes watering.

*If a recipe requires lots of chopped or grated onion (or cheese, carrot, fresh breadcrumbs etc.), you can use a food processor if you have one. For finely chopped garlic, onion or ginger use a cheese grater.

*To crush garlic, place the clove under the flat of a knife and press down hard.

Cooking

*Always make sure the water is boiling before adding rice or pasta to it.

*Try not to open the oven too often when cooking – this lowers the temperature and will affect the cooking time.

*Don't stir spaghetti and tagliatelle while it's cooking, as this will make it knotty when you come to serve it.

*Contrary to popular belief, you shouldn't prick sausages when you're frying or grilling them. This makes them spit fat and lose moisture.

fab ideas

✱ All-day breakfast

Breakfast doesn't have to take place at the crack of dawn – these tasty recipes can be enjoyed whenever you choose to emerge from the duvet! Boiled eggs are a comfort classic which take only a few minutes to cook, eggy bread can be sweet or savoury depending on your mood and baked egg and chips is the perfect hangover antidote.

✱ One-pot wonders

The great thing about these recipes is that they are all incredibly easy to prepare and can be cooked in one pot, which means you spend less time washing up afterwards. The sausage casserole is a particularly simple and delicious – perfect for feeding a gaggle of mates.

✱ TV dinners

Sometimes eating at the table is just too formal, or maybe you want to eat while watching your favourite soap. These meals are all ideal for eating in front of the box – as long as you don't mind greasy fingers!

✱ Brain food

When you're under pressure, it is tempting to rely on stimulants and quick fixes to get you through. Although these may give you an energy burst, they will then leave you flagging. To keep your concentration levels high, up your intake of:

Complex carbohydrates: brain fuels found in whole grains and vegetables.
Protein: improves ability to process information. Good sources are meat, fish, eggs and dairy products.
Omega-3 and omega-6 essential fatty acids: 'smart fats' vital for healthy brain cells. For omega-3 oils, eat oily fish (mackerel, herrings, sardines and kippers). Fresh brazil nuts, hazelnuts, almonds and sunflower seeds contain omega-6 oils.

cheap eats

4 **eggs**

4 slices **bread**

50 g (2 oz) **butter**

salt and **pepper**

PREP

COOK

SERVES

4

easy

cheap

fast

boiled eggs

Eggs are probably the ultimate in fast food, and are so easy to cook that you really can't go wrong.

1 Boil a saucepan of water then put the eggs into the pan with a spoon. Boil for 4–5 minutes – the whites should be set and the yolk lovely and runny.

2 Meanwhile, toast and butter the bread.

3 Crack open the eggs, sprinkle with salt and pepper and dip in the toast.

scrambled eggs with cheese and chilli sauce

Instead of making your own chilli sauce you can use a ready-made one. Alternatively, try adding some chopped fresh or canned tomato to a tub of guacamole.

PREP

15

COOK

20

SERVES

4

spicy

yum!

saucy

1 First make the chilli sauce. Put the red chillies, sugar, white wine vinegar and water in a saucepan and heat gently until the sugar has dissolved. Bring to the boil then turn down the heat and cook for 10 minutes, until it becomes thick and syrupy. Take off the heat, leave it to cool down, then stir in the lemon juice, coriander leaves and a dash of salt and pepper.

2 To make the scrambled eggs, beat the eggs in a bowl then stir in the onion, chilli, sweetcorn and a good dash of salt and pepper.

3 Melt the butter in a large saucepan then add the egg mix. Cook over a medium heat, stirring all the time, until the eggs are softly scrambled. Take the pan off the heat straight away and stir in the cheese. Dollop onto warm tortillas and chuck on the slices of green chilli, the coriander, chives and grated cheese and the sweet chilli sauce.

10 **eggs**

1 **onion**, finely chopped

1 **green chilli**, deseeded and finely chopped, plus extra to top

4 tablespoons **canned sweetcorn**

salt and **pepper**

25 g (1 oz) **butter**

75 g (3 oz) **Cheddar cheese**, grated, plus extra to top

8 **flour tortillas**, warmed

chopped **coriander** and **chives**, to sprinkle

Sweet Chilli Sauce:

4 **red chillies**, deseeded and finely chopped

50 g (2 oz) **sugar**

2 tablespoons **white wine vinegar**

6 tablespoons **water**

2 tablespoons **lemon juice**

4½ tablespoons **coriander leaves**, chopped

salt and **pepper**

4 **eggs**

salt and **pepper**

1 tablespoon **vegetable oil**

4 slices **bread**

eggy bread

Fried Eggy Bread makes a great hangover cure with grilled tomatoes or tomato ketchup; or if you are in need of a sugar fix add jam, honey or marmalade.

1 Crack the eggs into a bowl, sprinkle on some salt and pepper, and beat with a fork until smooth.

2 Heat the oil in a large frying pan. Dip a slice of bread into the egg mix so that it is covered, then place in the pan to fry, and do the same with the other bits of bread. Pour any leftover egg into the pan and cook until the bread is slightly brown on the bottom.

3 Separate the pieces of bread if they are stuck together, then flip them over and fry until brown on the other side. Drain on kitchen paper, then tuck in.

yum!

share

snack

basic omelette

There are loads of different fillings that you can add – try fried mushrooms and Cheddar cheese, chopped mixed chives, parsley and tarragon, or fried onion and bacon.

1 Crack the eggs into a bowl and beat well, then add the water and a dash of salt and pepper and beat again, but do not over-beat.

2 Melt the butter in a frying pan over a medium heat. When the butter starts to foam, but before it goes brown, tip in the eggs.

3 Leave for a few seconds then, using a fork or spoon, scrape the mixture away from the edge of the pan into the centre, so the egg runs to the sides. Do this a couple of times and the eggs will set. Cook for another 30 seconds until the bottom is golden but the top is still slightly runny and creamy. Add any fillings you like and then fold the omelette in half and you have an easy but tasty brunch.

PREP

COOK

SERVES

1

cheap

easy

fast

2 **eggs**

1 tablespoon **water**

salt and **pepper**

15 g (½ oz) **butter**

150 g (5 oz) **green beans**, cut into short bits

1 tablespoon **vegetable oil**

15 g (½ oz) **butter**

1 **red onion**, chopped

4 **eggs**

salt and **pepper**

25 g (1 oz) **chorizo sausage**, thinly sliced

50 g (2 oz) **Cheddar cheese**, grated

PREP

10

COOK

15

SERVES

2

fab

spicy

yum!

green bean and chorizo omelette

The spicy, garlicky chorizo sausage adds bucketloads of colour and bite to a simple omelette, but you can use any sausage, bacon, ham or pepperoni that you happen to have in your fridge.

1 Boil the green beans for 4 minutes, then drain.

2 Heat the oil and butter in a frying pan. Add the chopped onion and fry on a low heat for 3 minutes until soft. Beat the eggs and add them to the pan with a dash of salt and pepper. Fry on a low heat for 2–3 minutes until lightly set, pushing the cooked edges of the omelette towards the centre of the pan with a fork or spoon so the uncooked mixture runs to the side of the pan.

3 Scatter the green beans and chorizo over the top of the omelette and then sprinkle on the Cheddar. Put under a medium grill for about 2 minutes, until the cheese is bubbling away, then dig in.

toad-in-the-hole

Juicy sausages encased in a huge Yorkshire pudding – just perfect to have for a large lunch with a pint.

PREP
10

COOK
25

SERVES
4

1 Heat the oven to 220°C (425°F), Gas Mark 7.

2 Put the flour and a dash of salt and pepper into a bowl then crack in the egg. Slowly whisk in the milk and water until the batter is smooth and frothy.

3 Separate the sausages from each other. Stretch each rasher of bacon by running the flat edge of a knife along the rasher until it is half as long again. Wrap a rasher of bacon around each sausage.

4 Pour the oil into a roasting tin and add the bacon-wrapped sausages. Cook in the oven for 5 minutes until sizzling. Whisk the batter again.

5 Take the tin out of the oven and quickly pour in the batter. Put the tin back in the oven and cook for about 20 minutes until the batter has risen and is golden. Delicious with baked beans and mashed potatoes.

125 g (4 oz) **plain flour**

salt and **pepper**

1 **egg**

300 ml (½ pint) **milk**, or **milk mixed with water**

500 g (1 lb) **pork sausages**

8 **rindless bacon rashers**

2 tablespoons **vegetable oil**

mates

beer

share

8 **sausages**

2 **onions**, cut into wedges

Mustard mash:

1 kg (2 lb) **potatoes**, quartered but unpeeled

75 g (3 oz) **butter**

1–2 tablespoons **mustard**

1 **garlic clove**, crushed

salt and **pepper**

1 large bunch of **parsley**, chopped

dash of **olive oil**

yum!

easy

fast

sausages with mustard mash

Bangers and mash is one of the most comforting meals around. This is a great home-made version of traditional pub grub – but with a mustard kick.

1 First start the mash. Put the potatoes into a large saucepan of cold water, bring to the boil and simmer for 15 minutes.

2 Meanwhile, fry or grill the sausages on a medium heat for 10 minutes, turning to get an even colour. Add the onion wedges and cook with the sausages for 6–7 minutes.

3 Drain the potatoes well when they are cooked, and when they are cool enough to touch, peel them, then mash well so they are nice and creamy.

4 Add the butter, mustard, garlic and a good sprinkling of salt and pepper to the potatoes, and carry on mashing. Taste and add more mustard if you want. Finally, stir in the parsley and a dash of olive oil.

5 Pile the mash up on a plate and stick the sausages and onion wedges on top.

sausage casserole

Simple and cheap, you can make this in just one pot, which saves on the washing-up. For a meat-free alternative, use vegetarian sausages and stock and ditch the Worcestershire sauce.

1 Heat the oven to 180°C (350°F), Gas Mark 4.

2 Grill the sausages for 5 minutes, until brown but not completely cooked, then put them on a plate.

3 Heat the oil in an ovenproof dish, then fry the onion for 5 minutes, until slightly brown. Chuck in the carrots, celery and potatoes, then stir in the flour.

4 Add the beans, stock, Worcestershire sauce, tomato purée, mustard, sugar, and a dash of salt and pepper and bring to the boil. Chuck the sausages into the pan, cover, and cook in the oven for 1 hour then dish up.

PREP

15

COOK

75

SERVES

2

share

boozy

cheap

8 **chipolata sausages**

1 tablespoon **vegetable oil**

1 **onion**, chopped

3 **carrots**, peeled and cut into chunks

2 **celery sticks**, thickly sliced

2 small **baking potatoes**, quartered

1 tablespoon **plain flour**

400 g (13 oz) **can mixed beans**, drained and rinsed, or **baked beans**

300 ml (½ pint) **chicken stock**

1 tablespoon **Worcestershire sauce**

1 tablespoon **tomato purée**

2 teaspoons **mustard**

2 teaspoons **sugar**

salt and **pepper**

dinner jackets

1 **baking potato**

100 g (3½ oz) **cottage cheese**

2 tablespoons frozen **sweetcorn**, defrosted

¼ **green pepper**, cored, deseeded and cut into cubes

1 tablespoon **red onion**, chopped

salt and **pepper**

PREP

COOK

SERVES

Baked potatoes make a fantastic, cheap, low-fat meal and, even better, take no effort at all!

1 Heat the oven to 200°C (400°F), Gas Mark 6.

2 Prick the potato and bake in the oven for 1¼ hours, until cooked through and a bit squashy inside. Or, prick the potato, put it on a sheet of kitchen paper and microwave on full power for 6 minutes.

3 Meanwhile, mix the other ingredients.

4 Cut the potato in half and pile the cottage cheese mix on top.

Other toppings:

Mix a small, mashed avocado with 2 tablespoons of cottage cheese or fromage frais and sprinkle with crispy grilled bacon.

Mash a small 100 g (3½ oz) can of tuna or salmon with 3 tablespoons of cottage cheese or fromage frais, then stir in 1 chopped spring onion, ¼ chopped red pepper and some chopped cucumber.

Spicy Coleslaw (see page 76)

The old favourite – canned baked beans and cheese.

chilli con carne

One of Mexico's best-known exports, this spicy dish combines beef, beans and fiery chillies – add extra chilli powder to make it as hot as you can stand.

1 Heat the oil in a saucepan, chuck in the onions, red pepper and garlic and gently fry until soft. Add the meat and fry until just brown. Mix in the stock, and add the chilli powder, beans, tomatoes, cumin and a dash of salt and pepper.

2 Bring to the boil, then cover, lower the heat and simmer very gently for 50–60 minutes, stirring occasionally so it doesn't stick.

3 Meanwhile, boil the rice according to the packet instructions, then drain.

4 Pile up the rice, dollop on the cooked chilli and then the soured cream, and scatter over the chilli seeds, grated Cheddar and spring onion. Delicious!

PREP

COOK

SERVES

spicy

mates

share

2 tablespoons **vegetable oil**

3 **onions**, chopped

1 **red pepper**, cored, deseeded and cut into cubes

2 **garlic cloves**, crushed

500 g (1 lb) **beef mince**

450 ml (¾ pint) **beef stock**

½–1 teaspoon **chilli powder**

475 g (15 oz) **cooked red kidney beans**

400 g (13 oz) **can chopped tomatoes**

½ teaspoon **cumin**

salt and **pepper**

250 g (8 oz) **rice**

To serve:

soured cream

chilli seeds

Cheddar cheese, grated

spring onion, finely chopped

1 kg (2 lb) **beef mince**

salt and **pepper**

1 tablespoon **fresh mixed herbs**

2 teaspoons **Worcestershire sauce**

1–2 teaspoons **mustard**

To serve:

8 **burger buns**

8 **lettuce leaves**

ketchup or relishes

1 **onion**, sliced

4 **tomatoes**, sliced

COOK

10

SERVES

4

yum!

spicy

snack

spicy beefburgers

You can't beat a big, juicy burger, and if you want to make a cheeseburger just add any cheese you like – Cheddar, Stilton, Gruyère or Roquefort all work well.

1 Put the beef in a bowl and add a good dash of salt and pepper, then stir in the mixed herbs, Worcestershire sauce and mustard, and mix well. Divide into 8 flat burgers.

2 Cook the burgers under a medium grill for 3–5 minutes on each side, depending on how well cooked you like your beef.

3 Cut the buns in half. Put a lettuce leaf on top of each bun base, bung on a burger and some ketchup or relish. Put the onion and tomato slices on top, and finish up with the top of the bun. Make some home-made potato wedges (see page 78) or have a packet of crisps with them.

cottage pie

Cottage Pie is a real old-time favourite, but sometimes the old things are the best, as this epitome of comfort food proves.

1 Chop the onions, carrots and celery very finely. Heat half the butter and oil in a large saucepan, add the chopped vegetables and fry, stirring for 5 minutes until they start to soften. Add the meat and fry for another 5 minutes, breaking it up with a spoon.

2 Stir in the stock, ketchup, herbs and a little salt and pepper, and bring to the boil. Turn down the heat, cover, and simmer gently for 20 minutes, stirring occasionally.

3 Meanwhile, cut the potatoes into chunks and boil for 15–20 minutes. Drain, then mash well and stir in the milk and the rest of the butter.

4 Heat the oven to 200°C (400°F), Gas Mark 6.

5 Stir the baked beans into the meat mix. Turn into a large, shallow ovenproof dish or individual dishes. Spoon the potatoes over the top of the meat, spreading it right to the edges of the dish or dishes.

6 Bake for about 40 minutes until the potato is pale gold on top, then dish up with a couple of vegetables.

PREP

25

COOK

70

SERVES

4

keeps

fab

cheap

2 **onions**

4 medium-sized **carrots**

4 **celery sticks**

50 g (2 oz) **butter**

2 tablespoons **vegetable oil**

550 g (1 lb 2 oz) **lamb mince**

500 ml (17 fl oz) **chicken or lamb stock**

4 tablespoons **tomato ketchup**

½ teaspoon **dried mixed herbs**

salt and **pepper**

2 kg (4 lb) large **potatoes**, peeled

150 ml (¼ pint) **milk**

400 g (13 oz) **can baked beans**

pork stir-fry

2 tablespoons **vegetable oil**

2 **garlic cloves**, finely chopped

1 teaspoon grated **fresh root ginger**

1 **chilli**, deseeded and finely chopped

1 **red pepper**, cored, deseeded and cut into strips

3 **carrots**, cut into strips

1 large **onion**, sliced

250 g (8 oz) **pork**, cut into cubes

1 **courgette**, sliced

1 small **broccoli** head, divided into florets

Sauce:

2 tablespoons **soy sauce**

2 tablespoons **orange juice**

1 teaspoon **tomato purée**

1 teaspoon **vinegar**

1 teaspoon **brown sugar**

COOK

15

SERVES

4

fun

fresh

fast

Stir-fries are one of the tastiest and healthiest ways to eat vegetables, plus they're pretty cheap as you don't need to use much meat.

1 Heat the oil in a wok or large frying pan and add the garlic, ginger and chilli to warm them up but do not let them colour.

2 Chuck in the pepper, carrots, onion and pork and stir-fry over a medium to high heat for about 5 minutes then add the courgette and broccoli.

3 Stir in the sauce ingredients and let them bubble, then toss the ingredients through the sauce and stir-fry for a few more minutes. For a filling meal eat with rice or noodles.

pasta with tomato and bacon sauce

Just add warm, crusty garlic bread and a salad for a good, easy nosh.

1 Put the garlic, tomatoes, olive oil, mixed herbs and sugar into a saucepan. Add a dash of salt and pepper and bring to the boil, then cover and simmer for 10 minutes.

2 Add the bacon and simmer, uncovered, for another 5 minutes.

3 Stir in the mascarpone cheese or crème fraîche, heat up, then taste and add more salt and pepper if it needs it.

4 Meanwhile, cook the pasta according to the packet instructions.

5 Dollop the sauce over the pasta and enjoy with garlic bread and salad.

PREP

5

COOK

20

SERVES

4

easy

snack

saucy

2 **garlic cloves**, crushed

2 x 400 g (13 oz) **cans chopped tomatoes**

4 tablespoons **olive oil**

1 teaspoon **dried mixed herbs**

1 teaspoon **sugar**

salt and **pepper**

8 **rindless bacon rashers**, finely chopped

75 g (3 oz) **mascarpone cheese** or 75 ml (3 fl oz) **crème fraîche**

375 g (12 oz) **pasta**

potato and bacon gratin

posh

yum!

share

750 g–1 kg (1½–2 lb) **potatoes**, unpeeled

20 g (¾ oz) **butter**

4½ teaspoons **vegetable oil**

8 **rindless bacon rashers**, cut into strips

1 large **onion**, finely chopped

2 **garlic cloves**, crushed

25 g (1 oz) **mushrooms**, sliced

150–175 ml (5–6 fl oz) **double cream**

1 tablespoon **parsley**, finely chopped

salt and **pepper**

5 tablespoons **Cheddar cheese**, grated

3 tablespoons **Parmesan cheese**, grated

Ideally use Maris Piper or King Edward potatoes as these varieties will soak up the yummy juices like a sponge and make the sauce lovely and thick.

1 Heat the oven to 180°C (350°F), Gas Mark 4.

2 Cook the potatoes in a saucepan of boiling water for about 20 minutes, or until tender.

3 Meanwhile, melt half the butter with half the oil in a frying pan. Add the bacon and fry until it is starting to go brown, then drain on kitchen paper and put in an ovenproof dish.

4 Add the rest of the butter and oil and fry the onion and garlic over a medium heat for 5 minutes, stirring occasionally, until soft. Add the mushrooms and fry until all the vegetables are starting to go brown. Drain on kitchen paper, then put all the vegetables into the ovenproof dish. Mix well.

5 Drain the potatoes, cut into wedges then add them to the ovenproof dish. Mix the cream with the parsley, add a dash of salt and pepper, mix, and pour over the vegetables.

5 Mix the Cheddar and Parmesan cheeses together and scatter over the top. Bake in the oven for 20–30 minutes until crisp and golden. Eat on its own, or have with chicken for a bigger meal.

tuna and pasta bake

Almost everyone loves this fishy pasta dish. For a change, or if you want a vegetarian option, use tofu instead of tuna.

1 Cook the pasta according to the packet instructions.

2 Meanwhile, heat the oil in a large frying pan. Add the chopped onion and fry gently for 3 minutes. Add the peppers and garlic and carry on frying, stirring a lot, for 5 minutes. Stir in the tomatoes and fry for 1 minute until they are soft.

3 Melt the butter in another pan, toss in the breadcrumbs and stir until all the bread is covered in butter.

4 Drain the pasta, add the pepper and tomato mix, and then the tuna. Mix together, then put in an ovenproof dish.

5 Sprinkle the cheese and then the breadcrumbs over the pasta and cook under a medium grill for 3–5 minutes until the cheese has melted and the breadcrumbs are golden. Dish up with vegetables such as broccoli, green beans or carrots.

PREP

5

COOK

25

SERVES

2

easy

cheap

snack

250 g (8 oz) **pasta shells**

2 tablespoons **vegetable oil**

1 small **onion**, finely chopped

2 **red peppers**, cored, deseeded and cubed

1 **garlic clove**, crushed

150 g (5 oz) **cherry tomatoes**, cut in half

15 g (½ oz) **butter**

50 g (2 oz) **breadcrumbs**

400 g (13 oz) **can tuna**, drained and flaked

125 g (4 oz) **mozzarella or Gruyère cheese**, grated

250 g (8 oz) floury **potatoes** (like Maris Piper or King Edward), peeled and cut into cubes

400 g (13 oz) **can tuna**, drained and flaked

50 g (2 oz) **Cheddar cheese**, grated

4 **spring onions**, finely chopped

1 small **garlic clove**, crushed

2 teaspoons **dried thyme**

1 small **egg**, beaten

½ teaspoon **cayenne pepper**

salt and **pepper**

4 teaspoons **flour** flavoured with **salt** and **pepper**

vegetable oil, for frying

spicy tuna fish cakes

If you want to try something a little different, use canned red salmon instead of tuna, or liven up the mayonnaise by adding lemon juice, chilli, capers or chopped gherkins.

1 Boil the potatoes for 10 minutes, until tender. Drain, mash and leave to cool down.

2 Meanwhile, beat the tuna, cheese, spring onions, garlic, thyme and egg into the mashed potato and add a dash of cayenne, salt and pepper.

3 Divide the mixture into four and make into thick burgers. Sprinkle the flour over them and fry in a shallow layer of hot oil for 5 minutes on each side, until they are crisp and golden. Eat with a mixed green salad.

snack

telly

posh

tuna kedgeree

PREP

10

COOK

25

SERVES

4

fast

cheap

easy

Kedgeree was a typical Victorian breakfast dish, but don't let that put you off as this modern take makes a great lunch or supper. Try it – you'll love it.

1 Cook the rice according to the packet instructions. Add the broad beans and cook for another 3 minutes, then drain.

2 Meanwhile, hard-boil the eggs. Put the eggs in a saucepan of cold water. Bring them to the boil and simmer for 6–7 minutes, then cool in cold water.

3 Flake the tuna into small chunks, then take the shell off the eggs and cut them lengthways into quarters.

4 Melt the butter in a large frying pan, add the onion and curry paste and fry gently for 3 minutes. Add the drained rice, broad beans, tuna and eggs.

5 Stir in the parsley and add a dash of salt and pepper. Stir gently over a low heat for 1 minute, then toss on a couple of lemon or lime wedges and tuck in.

250 g (8 oz) **basmati rice**

100 g (3½ oz) frozen **baby broad beans**

4 **eggs**

400 g (13 oz) **can tuna**, drained

25 g (1 oz) **butter**

1 small **onion**, finely chopped

1 teaspoon **medium curry paste**

small handful of **parsley**, chopped

salt and **pepper**

lemon or lime wedges, to top

125 g (4 oz) **plain flour**

pinch of **salt**

1 **egg**, lightly beaten

300 ml (½ pint) **milk**

vegetable oil or butter,
for greasing the pan

basic pancakes

These are a great thing to cook for friends, and a good laugh to make if everyone tosses their own pancakes.

1 Put the flour and salt into a bowl and make a hole in the centre. Pour the egg and a little of the milk into the hole. Whisk well, slowly adding the milk to make a smooth paste. Whisk in the rest of the milk. Pour into a jug or pint glass.

easy

2 Put a little oil or butter into a medium-sized frying pan and heat until it starts to smoke. Pour off any excess oil and pour a little batter into the pan, tilting the pan until the base is coated in a thin layer. Cook for 1–2 minutes until the bottom goes golden.

3 Flip the pancake over and cook for another 30–45 seconds until golden on the second side. Fill with a savoury or sweet concoction.

fast

mates

ham and cheese pancakes

These make a tasty lunch or supper – just serve with a salad and your friends are bound to be impressed.

1 Heat the oven to 200°C (400°F), Gas Mark 6.

2 Make the pancakes and leave to cool while you make the filling.

3 Melt the butter or margarine in a saucepan over a low heat, then add the flour. Cook for 2 minutes, stirring all the time. Gradually add the milk and bring the sauce to the boil, stirring constantly. Simmer gently for 2–3 minutes. Take the pan off the heat, and add a good dash of salt and pepper. Stir in the ham and cheese.

4 Divide the ham and cheese sauce among the pancakes, putting it in a sausage-shape in the centre of each pancake, then roll up and put in a shallow ovenproof dish. Bake for 15 minutes and eat while hot.

PREP

20

COOK

25

SERVES

4

snack

yum!

fab

1 quantity **Basic Pancakes** (see opposite)

vegetable oil, for greasing the pan

Cheese sauce:

50 g (2 oz) **butter or margarine**

40 g (1½ oz) **plain flour**

600 ml (1 pint) **milk**

salt and **pepper**

300 g (10 oz) **sliced ham**

175 g (6 oz) **Cheddar cheese**, grated

2 tablespoons **vegetable oil**

1 **onion**, chopped

1 **garlic clove**, crushed

125 g (4 oz) **mushrooms**, sliced

1 tablespoon **plain flour**

300 ml (½ pint) **chicken stock**

500 g (1 lb) **cooked chicken**, cut into cubes

1 tablespoon chopped **parsley**

salt and **pepper**

375 g (12 oz) **puff pastry**, thawed if frozen

1 **egg**, beaten, for brushing

posh

yum!

mates

chicken and mushroom pie

Pies may seem rather scary to make, but if you buy ready-made puff pastry then you can knock this up in no time at all.

1 Heat the oven to 200°C (400°F), Gas Mark 6.

2 Heat the oil in a frying pan. Add the onion and fry over a medium heat, stirring occasionally, until soft. Add the garlic and mushrooms and cook for 2 minutes.

3 Take the pan off the heat and stir in the flour. Slowly add the stock and stir until well mixed. Put back on the heat and bring to the boil, stirring until it is thick and smooth.

4 Stir in the cooked chicken, parsley and some salt and pepper. Mix well, then put in a 1.2 litre (2 pint) pie dish or similar-sized ovenproof dish.

5 Roll out the pastry to a shape just larger than the dish and put it over the pie. Push down the edges to seal them then cut off any extra pasty. Prick some holes in the lid with a fork, brush with beaten egg and bake for 30 minutes, until golden.

chicken and vegetable pies

PREP

20

COOK

30

MAKES

10

telly

beer

snack

These tasty, flaky little pies are great for snacking on, or to have with a mound of creamy mashed potato and carrots for a filling meal.

50 g (2 oz) **butter**

2 large boneless, skinless **chicken breasts**, cut into cubes

1 large **leek**, trimmed and chopped

150 g (5 oz) **carrots**, thinly sliced

2 teaspoons **plain flour**

200 ml (7 fl oz) **chicken stock**

100 g (3½ oz) **green beans**, sliced

4 tablespoons **double cream**

175 g (6 oz) **ready-made filo pastry**

1 Melt half the butter in a large frying pan and fry the chicken for 3 minutes until it starts to go brown. Chuck in the leek and carrots and fry for 2 minutes until the leeks go soft, then stir in the flour.

2 Stir in the stock, drop in the green beans and bring to the boil, stirring. Cover and cook gently for 5 minutes. Turn off the heat, stir in the cream and leave to cool.

3 Heat the oven to 200°C (400°F), Gas Mark 6.

4 Melt the rest of the butter. Cut the pastry into thirty 12 cm (5 inch) squares. Brush one square with melted butter, cover with another square and brush with butter again. Add a third square and brush the edges with butter. Put a spoonful of the chicken mix in the centre. Bring up the corners of the pastry to meet and pinch the edges together to make an envelope shape. Do the same thing with the rest of the filling and pastry to make 10 pies.

5 Put the pies on a greased baking sheet and brush with the rest of the butter. Bake for 15–20 minutes, or until golden brown, then eat while hot.

16 **chicken drumsticks**

4 tablespoons **honey**

finely grated rind and juice of 1 **lemon**

finely grated rind and juice of 1 **orange**

3 tablespoons **Worcestershire sauce**

4 tablespoons **tomato ketchup**

PREP

COOK

MAKES

gooey

fun

party

sticky chicken drumsticks

This is such an easy way to liven up chicken. The drumsticks are best eaten with your fingers; who cares how messy they are, as they taste so good!

1 Heat the oven to 180°C (350°F), Gas Mark 4.

2 Make a few diagonal cuts in the fleshy bit of each chicken drumstick and put them in a single layer in a roasting tin or other oven-proof dish.

3 Mix together the rest of the ingredients and spoon over the chicken.

4 Cook in the oven for about 50 minutes, turning the drumsticks and spooning the juices over them a few times so that they are covered in the sticky glaze and don't burn. Eat them hot or cold – but definitely with your fingers.

chicken dippers with salsa

Grab a cold beer and snack on these – you can add chillies to the salsa if you want to spice it up, or have some soured cream or guacamole to dip into as well. Perfect food to slob out on the sofa with.

1 First, make the salsa, cut the tomatoes and cucumber into tiny pieces about the size of the sweetcorn and mix them all together in a bowl, then mix in the coriander.

2 Cut the chicken into long, finger-like slices.

3 Beat the eggs, milk and a little salt and pepper together in a bowl.

4 Mix the breadcrumbs with the Parmesan.

5 Dip one chicken strip into the egg, then roll in the breadcrumbs. Carry on doing this until all the chicken strips are well covered.

6 Heat the butter and oil in a large frying pan and add the chicken slices. Cook for 5–6 minutes, turning a few times until they are brown all over. Then just dip into the salsa and munch away.

PREP

20

COOK

8

SERVES

2–3

mates

fab

snack

4 boneless, skinless **chicken breasts**

2 **eggs**

2 tablespoons **milk**

salt and **pepper**

100 g (3½ oz) **breadcrumbs**

4 tablespoons **Parmesan cheese**, grated

25 g (1 oz) **butter**

2 tablespoons **vegetable oil**

Salsa:

2 **tomatoes**

¼ **cucumber**

75 g (3 oz) **sweetcorn**, defrosted if frozen

1 tablespoon **coriander leaves**, chopped

250 g (8 oz) **macaroni**

Cheese sauce:

50 g (2 oz) **butter or margarine**

40 g (1½ oz) **plain flour**

600 ml (1 pint) **milk**

salt and **pepper**

175 g (6 oz) **Cheddar cheese**, grated

easy

cheap

share

macaroni cheese

This has to be one of the easiest meals to make, plus it is cheap and you are likely to already have everything at home. Perfect for when you can't be bothered to go to the shops.

1 Cook the macaroni according to the packet instructions. Drain and put on one side.

2 Melt the butter or margarine in a saucepan over a low heat, then add the flour. Cook for 2 minutes, stirring all the time. Gradually add the milk, and bring the sauce to the boil, stirring constantly. Simmer gently for 2–3 minutes. Take the pan off the heat, and add lots of salt and pepper.

3 Add the cooked macaroni and most of the Cheddar cheese to the sauce and mix well. Pour into an ovenproof dish and sprinkle the rest of the cheese over the top. Brown under a hot grill and dish up while nice and hot.

classic tomato pizza

Irresistibly tasty, these pizzas will be a hit with housemates and friends. There are countless topping variations you can try. (See pages 102–103 for some great ideas.)

PREP

20

COOK

10

MAKES

4

party

yum!

telly

4 **ready-to-cook pizza bases**

3 tablespoons **olive oil**

2 **red onions**, finely sliced

2 **garlic cloves**, crushed and chopped

2 x 400 g (13 oz) **cans chopped tomatoes**

1 teaspoon **red wine vinegar**

pinch of **sugar**

salt and **pepper**

8 **anchovy fillets**, cut into thin lengths

2 tablespoons **black olives**, pitted

1 tablespoon **capers**

250 g (8 oz) **mozzarella cheese**, sliced

1 Heat the oven to 230°C (450°F), Gas Mark 8.

2 Heat the oil in a large saucepan, add the onion and garlic and fry for 3 minutes. Add the tomatoes, vinegar, sugar, and a dash of salt and pepper. Turn the heat up and simmer until the mixture has shrunk down by half to make a thick and rich tomato sauce.

3 Put the pizza bases on baking sheets, spoon over the sauce and spread to the edge with the back of a spoon.

4 Chuck all the toppings onto the pizza – the anchovies, olives and capers first, and then the sliced mozzarella. Cook in the oven for 10 minutes until sizzling and golden.

soups and stuff

1 tablespoon **vegetable oil**

1 kg (2 lb) **tomatoes**, roughly chopped

1 small **onion**, chopped

1 **orange**

1 **sugar cube**

1.8 litres (3 pints) **chicken or vegetable stock**

dried mixed herbs

salt and **pepper**

share

fresh

keeps

fresh tomato soup

This tomato soup is not only dead easy to make, but it is also delicious with its subtle orange flavour which makes it taste really different to the usual tomato soup.

1 Heat the oil in a frying pan. Add the tomatoes and onions and fry for about 8 minutes until they are soft.

2 Peel the rind off the orange and rub the sugar cube over the rind, to absorb the zest, then add the cube with the stock to the tomato mixture. Squeeze in the juice from the orange, bring to the boil, cover and simmer gently for 25 minutes.

3 Squash the soup through a fine sieve with a spoon. Heat up again, add some mixed herbs, salt and pepper if you want, and serve with warm, crusty bread.

mushroom soup with crispy bacon

This is a superbly rich and decadent soup. Cook it for someone you fancy – you can't fail to impress them!

PREP

COOK

SERVES

snack

yum!

posh

4 rashers **rindless bacon,** finely chopped

50 g (2 oz) **butter**

1 **onion**, finely chopped

1 **garlic clove**, finely chopped

375 g (12 oz) **mushrooms**, finely chopped

2 tablespoons **plain flour**

600 ml (1 pint) **vegetable or chicken stock**

150 ml (¼ pint) **milk**

salt and **pepper**

1 tablespoon **sherry**

150 ml (¼ pint) **double or whipping cream**

chopped **parsley,** to sprinkle

1 Fry the bacon pieces in a frying pan until they are crisp, then drain on kitchen paper and set aside.

2 Melt the butter in a large saucepan and fry the onion, garlic and mushrooms until soft and starting to colour. Sprinkle on the flour and stir so that it's well mixed together. Gradually pour on the stock and the milk, stirring well to mix. Bring to the boil, then turn down the heat and simmer for about 15–20 minutes.

3 Add salt and pepper, along with the sherry (if you have it), and half the cream. Heat the soup up, then pour into bowls.

4 Meanwhile, whip the rest of the cream until it is firm.

5 Spoon a little of the whipped cream on top of each bowl of soup. Sprinkle with the bacon pieces and parsley if you have it.

chunky carrot and lentil soup

2 tablespoons **vegetable oil**

1 large **onion**, chopped

2 **celery sticks**, sliced

500 g (1 lb) **carrots**, sliced

1 **garlic clove**, crushed

150 g (5 oz) **split red lentils**, rinsed

1.5 litres (2½ pints) **vegetable stock**

salt and **pepper**

Spiced butter:

40 g (1½ oz) **butter,** softened

2 **spring onions**, trimmed and finely chopped

¼ teaspoon **dried chilli flakes**

1 teaspoon **cumin seeds**, lightly crushed

finely grated rind of 1 **lemon**

small handful of **coriander leaves**, chopped

several **mint** sprigs, chopped

PREP
10

COOK
40

SERVES
4

mates

fab

spicy

This nutritious soup makes a fab meal if you serve it with some good grainy bread. A zesty, spiced butter, stirred in at the end, adds another dimension to the taste.

1 First make the spiced butter, if you want it. Put all the ingredients in a bowl and beat together until they are well mixed. Then put in the fridge until you need it.

2 To make the soup, heat the oil in a large saucepan. Add the onion and celery and cook gently for 5 minutes until soft. Add the carrots and garlic and fry for another 3 minutes.

3 Add the lentils and stock and bring just to the boil. Turn down the heat, cover the pan and cook gently for 20–25 minutes until the vegetables are soft and the soup is pulpy.

4 Sprinkle with salt and pepper and let your friends add the spiced butter if they like it.

french onion soup

This is true comfort food, and tastes so good that your friends will be delighted if you cook it for them. *Bon Appetit!*

1 Melt the butter in a large saucepan and add the onions and sugar. Turn down the heat so it is just simmering and cook the onions very slowly for 20–30 minutes until they are soft and a really deep golden brown. Stir occasionally and be careful that they do not burn.

2 Stir the flour into the onion mixture and cook over a very low heat for about 5 minutes, stirring lots so it doesn't burn or stick to the bottom of the pan.

3 Add the stock and a dash of salt and pepper. Turn up the heat so that the soup boils, stir all the time, then turn down the heat and simmer for 15–20 minutes. Taste the soup and add more salt and pepper if you want.

4 Meanwhile, toast the slices of French stick. Put a piece of toast in each bowl and sprinkle with grated Gruyère. Spoon the hot soup over the bread and sprinkle the parsley over the top.

PREP

15

COOK

60

SERVES

4

posh

snack

yum!

50 g (2 oz) **butter**

750 g (1½ lb) **onions**, thinly sliced

2 teaspoons **sugar**

2 teaspoons **plain flour**

1 litre (1¾ pints) **chicken or beef stock**

salt and **pepper**

½ small **French stick**, cut into 4 slices

50 g (2 oz) **Gruyère cheese**, grated

parsley, chopped, to sprinkle

50 g (2 oz) **split red lentils**

2 tablespoons **vegetable oil**

1 **onion**, finely chopped

2 **spring onions**, chopped

400 g (13 oz) **can plum tomatoes**

2 tablespoons **tomato purée**

2 tablespoons **fresh mixed herbs**, chopped

1.5 litres (2½ pints) hot **vegetable stock**

salt and **pepper**

75 g (3 oz) **small pasta shapes**

cheap

share

easy

tomato and lentil soup

A healthy, filling soup for a cold winter's day – comfort food at its best. Serve with chunks of bread for dunking.

1 Heat the oil in a large saucepan, add the onion and half the spring onions and fry for 5 minutes or until soft.

2 Add the lentils to the onions, then add the tomatoes, tomato purée and herbs. Pour in enough stock so the lentils are covered. Bring to the boil, turn down the heat and simmer for 20–25 minutes, or until soft, adding more stock if you need to.

3 Push the soup through a sieve to make it smoother, then put it back in the pan and stir in a dash of salt and pepper. Add some more of the stock if you think the soup is a little too thick. Bring back to the boil, add the pasta, lower the heat and simmer for 8–12 minutes, then slurp!

minestrone

PREP

15

COOK

35

SERVES

4

This hearty soup makes a great lunch. A sure way to warm you up on a cold day.

1 Heat the oil in a large saucepan and add the garlic and onion. Fry for 3 minutes, stirring all the time until soft but not brown.

2 Add the bacon, carrots, leek and chopped tomatoes to the pan and cook over a medium heat for 10 minutes, stirring now and then, until the vegetables are soft. Add the tomato purée and herbs and stir well.

3 Slowly stir in the beef stock and pasta shapes. Add a good dash of salt and pepper. Bring to the boil, lower the heat and simmer for 20 minutes. Sprinkle some Parmesan cheese over the top and enjoy.

mates

yum!

snack

1 tablespoon **vegetable oil**

1 **garlic clove**, crushed

1 **onion**, finely chopped

50 g (2 oz) **rindless streaky bacon**, chopped

2 **carrots**, finely chopped

1 small **leek**, sliced finely

400 g (13 oz) **can chopped tomatoes**

2 tablespoons **tomato purée**

1 tablespoon **dried mixed herbs**

1.2 litres (2 pints) **beef stock**

75 g (3 oz) **small pasta shapes**

salt and **pepper**

1 tablespoon **Parmesan cheese**, grated

25 g (1 oz) **butter**

2 large **leeks**, finely sliced

250 g (8 oz) **potatoes**, peeled and roughly chopped

1 **onion**, roughly chopped

750 ml (1¼ pints) **chicken stock or water**

300 ml (½ pint) **milk**

salt and **pepper**

PREP

COOK

SERVES

leek and potato soup

A good, traditional soup to curl up on the sofa with while watching TV. What a winner!

1 Melt the butter in a large saucepan, add the leeks, potatoes and onion. Stir well so they are covered in the butter. Cook over a very low heat for about 15 minutes, until the vegetables are soft, stirring to stop them from becoming brown.

2 Add the chicken stock or water and milk, and a dash of salt and pepper. Bring to the boil, then turn down the heat and simmer gently for about 20 minutes until all the vegetables are tender.

3 Push the soup through a sieve to make it smoother.

4 Add more salt and pepper if needed, and heat until very hot, then eat straight away.

chilli bean and carrot soup

This warming soup has a hint of chilli, which can give it a bit of a kick.

1 Heat the oil in a large saucepan, add the onion and fry for 5 minutes, until slightly brown. Chuck in the carrots, red pepper and garlic and fry for another 3 minutes, until soft. Stir in the chilli and cumin and cook for 1 more minute.

2 Add the kidney beans, passata, stock and sugar and a dash of salt and pepper. Bring to the boil, then cover and simmer for 30 minutes, until thick.

3 Dish up, then dollop on a spoonful of Greek yogurt and sprinkle some paprika and cumin seeds over the top.

PREP

10

COOK

40

SERVES

4

spicy

mates

posh

1 tablespoon **olive oil**

1 **onion**, chopped

2 **carrots**, about 250 g (8 oz), cut into cubes

1 **red pepper**, cored, deseeded and cut into cubes

2 **garlic cloves**, chopped

1 small fresh or dried **red chilli**, deseeded and chopped

1 teaspoon **cumin seeds**

400 g (13 oz) **can red kidney beans**, drained and rinsed

500 g (1 lb) **passata**

600 ml (1 pint) **vegetable or chicken stock**

1 tablespoon **sugar**

salt and **pepper**

To top:
Greek yogurt
paprika
cumin seeds

1.2 litres (2 pints) **chicken stock**

1 **star anise**

7 cm (3 inch) piece of **cinnamon stick**, broken up

2 **garlic cloves**, finely chopped

125 ml (4 fl oz) **Thai fish sauce**

8 **coriander roots**, finely chopped

4 teaspoons **light brown sugar**

4 teaspoons **light soy sauce**

200 g (7 oz) **skinless chicken**, cut into cubes

125 g (4 oz) **green vegetables**, such as spring cabbage, chard or pak choi, roughly chopped

50 g (2 oz) **bean sprouts**

200 g (7 oz) **rice sticks**, cooked

15 g (½ oz) **coriander leaves**

PREP

10

COOK

12

SERVES

4

fresh

fun

fab

chicken noodle soup

If you don't have all the ingredients for this soup, then it's a good reason to visit your nearest Chinese supermarket.

1 Put the chicken stock, star anise, cinnamon, garlic, fish sauce, coriander, sugar and soy sauce into a large saucepan and bring slowly to the boil.

2 Add the chicken cubes and simmer gently for 4 minutes.

3 Add the green vegetables and bean sprouts and simmer for 2 minutes.

4 Divide the rice sticks between four bowls, pour over the soup and sprinkle the coriander leaves on top.

vegetable and lentil soup

spicy

easy

cheap

This budget soup makes a really healthy, low-calorie lunch, and is a good way to use up any vegetables that need eating.

1 Heat the oil in a saucepan, add the onion and fry for 5 minutes, stirring until soft. Add the butter and vegetables and fry for 5 more minutes, stirring all the time.

2 Put in the turmeric and curry paste and cook for 1 minute, then add the stock and lentils and sprinkle with salt and pepper. Bring to the boil, cover and simmer for 40 minutes until the lentils are soft, then eat with bread.

1 tablespoon **vegetable oil**

1 **onion**, finely chopped

15 g (½ oz) **butter**

2 **carrots**, about 250 g (8 oz), finely chopped

1 **potato**, about 250 g (8 oz), finely chopped

1 **parsnip**, about 250 g (8 oz), finely chopped

¼ teaspoon **turmeric**

3 teaspoons **mild curry paste**

1.2 litres (2 pints) **vegetable or chicken stock**

75 g (3 oz) **split red lentils**, rinsed

salt and **pepper**

4 thick slices **bread**

4 slices **ham**

2 **tomatoes**, sliced

4 **eggs**

1 tablespoon **white wine vinegar**

3 tablespoons **crème fraîche**

2 tablespoons **fresh herbs**, chopped

salt and **pepper**

PREP

5

COOK

12

SERVES

2

easy

fast

yum!

tasty open toasties

A posh brunch – whip this up and enjoy with a large coffee and trashy Sunday papers.

1 Toast the bread on both sides, then top each piece with a slice of ham and 2 slices of tomato.

2 To poach the eggs, bring a large saucepan of water to the boil, add the vinegar, then stir the water rapidly in a circular motion so that you make a whirlpool. Break an egg into the centre of the pan. Cook for 3 minutes then remove from the pan and keep warm. Repeat with the rest of the eggs, then put 1 egg on each piece of toast.

3 Mix together the crème fraîche and herbs, add a dash of salt and pepper and dollop over the toasties.

club sandwich

PREP

10

COOK

10

SERVES

2

snack

mates

fab

6 rashers **bacon**

6 slices **bread**

6 tablespoons **mayonnaise**

8 **lettuce** leaves

salt and **pepper**

2 slices cooked **turkey**

2 **tomatoes**, thinly sliced

This famous American sandwich tradition-ally has three layers of white bread with turkey, but use brown bread and chicken if you prefer.

1 Cook the bacon in a large frying pan for 5–7 minutes, turning once, until crisp on both sides, then drain on kitchen paper.

2 Toast the bread on both sides, then spread one side of each slice with 1 tablespoon of mayonnaise.

3 Put two lettuce leaves on each of two slices of toast and sprinkle with salt and pepper.

4 Put one slice of turkey on top of the lettuce on each sandwich base, then top with another slice of toast, with the mayonnaise side facing up. Put the rest of the lettuce leaves on top and add the tomato slices, then the crispy bacon.

5 Cover with the other two slices of toast, mayonnaise side facing down. Leave the sandwiches whole, or cut into four triangles, and pierce with long toothpicks for the American diner look.

50 g (2 oz) **butter**, softened

4 slices white **bread**

2 slices **Cheddar cheese**

pepper

2 slices cooked **ham**

3 tablespoons **vegetable oil**

croque monsieur

This classic French dish was first served in a café in Paris in 1910 and has been popular ever since. You can use slices of chicken instead of ham, if preferred.

1 Spread half the butter over only one side of all the bread. Put a slice of cheese on two of the buttered slices, top with a slice of ham and sprinkle with pepper. Top with the remaining slices of bread, butter side down, pressing down hard.

2 Melt the rest of the butter with the oil in a large frying pan, and fry the croques until golden brown, turning once.

posh

yum!

fast

croque madame

It's surprising how much tastier this is than a basic cheese and bacon sandwich, when all you do differently is stick it in the oven!

4 rashers **bacon**

8 slices white **bread**, crusts removed

1–2 teaspoons **mustard**

125 g (4 oz) **Cheddar cheese**, finely grated

2 **tomatoes**, thinly sliced

40 g (1½ oz) **butter**, melted

1 Heat the oven to 230°C (450°F), Gas Mark 8.

2 Fry the bacon until brown.

3 Thinly spread half the slices of bread with mustard. Top these with the cheese, bacon and tomato slices divided equally among them. Cover with the rest of the slices of bread, pressing down hard.

4 Put the sandwiches on a baking sheet and brush the tops with half of the butter. Bake for about 5 minutes, or until slightly brown.

5 Turn over the sandwiches and brush with the rest of the butter. Bake for another 3–5 minutes and eat while hot.

easy

fast

fab

2 **eggs**

4 tablespoons **milk**

4 slices **bread**, crusts removed

2 tablespoons **olive oil**

75 g (3 oz) **cherry tomatoes**, cut in half

50 g (2 oz) **Cheddar cheese**, finely grated

PREP

COOK

SERVES

yum!

snack

posh

french toast sandwiches

This savoury dish is so simple to knock up. You can also make a sweet version – once the bread is cooked, soften some sliced apple, pear or banana in the pan, sprinkle the French toasts lightly with sugar and sandwich together with the fruit.

1 In a bowl, beat the eggs with the milk and tip into a large shallow dish. Soak the bread in the egg mixture, leave for a few moments, then turn the slices over and leave until the egg mixture has been absorbed.

2 Heat the oil in a large frying pan. Add the slices of bread and fry gently for about 1 minute until golden underneath. Turn the slices over and fry for 1 more minute. Drain on kitchen paper.

3 Add the tomatoes to the pan, stirring gently for about 30 seconds until warm. Put two French toasts on each plate and scatter with the tomatoes. Put the other two French toasts on top and sprinkle with the cheese.

grilled chicken sandwich

An easy lunch, but full of protein, so it will set you up for the rest of the day.

1 Heat the oil in a frying pan, add the onion and fry for 2–3 minutes, until beginning to soften.

2 Add the chicken and fry for 4–5 minutes, until it is brown and cooked through. Stir in the yogurt and a dash of pepper.

3 Fill the bread with the chicken and rocket, sprinkle with salt and serve.

PREP

5

COOK

10

SERVES

2

beer

telly

cool

1 tablespoon **vegetable oil**

1 **onion**, sliced

2 boneless, skinless **chicken breasts**, sliced

2 tablespoons **yogurt**

salt and **pepper**

1 **French stick**, quartered and split along one side

60 g (2½ oz) **rocket**

4 slices **bread**

2–3 **garlic cloves**, peeled and cut in half

8 tablespoons **olive oil**

salt

party

easy

share

garlic bread

The perfect accompaniment to Spaghetti Bolognese (see page 136) or Lasagne (see page 99 or 137).

1 Toast the bread on both sides under a medium grill until golden. While the bread is still warm, rub one side with the cut sides of the garlic.

2 Put the bread on a plate and drizzle 2 tablespoons of olive oil over each slice. Sprinkle with salt and have as a starter, snack, or with any pasta dish or salad.

bruschetta with tomatoes and anchovies

Bruschetta – Italian garlic bread – is a delicious starter. Eat it while hot, though, otherwise the toast will go soggy.

PREP

5

COOK

5

SERVES

4

fast

posh

snack

6 **tomatoes**

8 slices **ciabatta bread**

2 **garlic cloves**, peeled

small handful **parsley**, chopped

salt

olive oil, to drizzle

16 **anchovies**

1 Cut a cross at the stem end of each tomato. Put the tomatoes in a bowl and pour boiling water over to cover. Leave for 1–2 minutes, then drain and peel off the skins. Dice the tomatoes and put to one side.

2 Toast the bread on both sides under a medium grill until golden brown.

3 Rub the garlic over one side of the bread; the bread acts as a grater and the garlic is evenly spread over the bread.

4 Sprinkle the bruschetta with the parsley and salt and drizzle with olive oil. Spoon on the chopped tomatoes, then lay a couple of anchovies on top of each piece.

2 tablespoons **tomato ketchup**

4 teaspoons **balsamic** or **wine vinegar**

2 **muffins**, split

100 g (3½ oz) **can tuna**, drained and flaked

small handful of fresh **baby spinach leaves**, about 25 g (1 oz)

2 small **tomatoes**, thinly sliced

snack

griddled tuna muffins

Far more exciting than a normal sandwich, these toasted split muffins are filled with a tangy tuna salad to make a delicious kind of fish burger.

1 Mix together the tomato ketchup and vinegar and spread over the cut surfaces of the muffins.

2 Pile the tuna onto the muffin bases and scatter over the spinach. Add the tomato slices, then the muffin tops and press down firmly to make them compact.

3 Place the muffins under the grill and gently toast on both sides, turning carefully. Eat while warm.

baked tortillas with hummus

PREP

5

COOK

12

SERVES

4

A healthy but tasty way to snack. Grab a video and a bottle of wine and have a lovely night in while munching happily on these.

1 Heat the oven to 200°C (400°F), Gas Mark 6.

2 Cut each tortilla into 8 triangles, put on a baking sheet and brush with a little oil. Bake for 10–12 minutes until golden and crisp. Remove from the oven.

3 Meanwhile, put the chickpeas, garlic, yogurt and lemon juice in a bowl and mix really well until smooth and mushy. Sprinkle with salt and pepper, stir in the coriander and sprinkle with paprika. Then dip in the warm tortillas. Lovely!

yum!

posh

share

4 small **wheat tortillas**

1 tablespoon **olive oil**

Hummus:

400 g (13 oz) **can chickpeas**, drained and rinsed

1 **garlic clove**, chopped

4 tablespoons **yogurt**

2 tablespoons **lemon juice**

salt and **pepper**

1 tablespoon **coriander leaves**, chopped

paprika

spring rolls

250 g (8 oz) **spring roll wrappers**, each 12 cm (5 inches) square

1 **egg**, beaten

vegetable oil, for deep-frying

red chilli strips and **basil leaves**, to garnish

Filling:

2 tablespoons **vegetable oil**

2 **garlic cloves**, chopped

125 g (4 oz) **crab meat**

125 g (4 oz) **raw prawns**, peeled and chopped

125 g (4 oz) **pork mince**

pepper

125 g (4 oz) **vermicelli**, soaked and cut into 1 cm (½ inch) lengths

125 g (4 oz) **mushrooms**, chopped

2 tablespoons **Thai fish sauce**

2 tablespoons **soy sauce**

1 teaspoon **sugar**

5 **spring onions**, finely chopped

PREP

25

COOK

20

SERVES
6

yum!

party

mates

Spring rolls should be really crispy on the outside but soft inside, so make sure the oil is very hot and don't cook too many at once. These ones are best eaten dipped in a sweet chilli sauce.

1 First make the filling. Heat the oil in a wok and stir-fry the garlic for 1 minute.

2 Add the crab meat, prawns and pork, sprinkle with pepper and stir-fry for 10–12 minutes, or until lightly cooked.

3 Add the vermicelli, mushrooms, fish sauce, soy sauce, sugar and spring onions, and stir-fry for 5 minutes until all the liquid has been absorbed. Leave to cool.

4 Separate the spring roll wrappers and arrange them on a clean work surface. Cover with a clean tea towel to keep them soft. Put about 2 tablespoons of the filling on each wrapper, and brush the left and right edges with beaten egg. Fold the sides over the filling then roll up the wrappers like a sausage. Brush the top edge with more beaten egg and then seal. Keep the filled rolls covered while you make the rest.

5 Heat the oil in a wok and cook the spring rolls a few at a time, for 5–8 minutes, or until golden brown, turning them once. Drain on kitchen paper, top with chilli and basil.

vegetable samosas

If you're a fan of Indian food, then these crisp, savoury treats will become a dead-cert favourite.

1 Heat the oven to 200°C (400°F), Gas Mark 6.

2 In a large bowl, mix together the potatoes, peas, cumin, amchoor, chillies, onion, coriander, mint and lemon juice. Add a dash of salt and pepper.

3 Fold each sheet of filo pastry in half lengthways. Put a large spoonful of the potato mixture at one end and then fold the corner of the pastry over the mixture, covering it to make a triangular shape. Continue folding over the triangle of pastry along the length of the pastry strip to make a neat triangular samosa.

4 Make 11 more samosas in the same way, dividing the mixture evenly.

5 Put the samosas on a baking sheet, brush with melted butter, and bake for 15–20 minutes, or until golden.

PREP

10

COOK

15

MAKES

12

spicy

share

fab

3 large **potatoes**, boiled, peeled and roughly mashed

100 g (3½ oz) cooked **peas**

1 teaspoon **cumin seeds**

1 teaspoon **amchoor** (dried mango powder)

2 fresh **green chillies**, deseeded and finely chopped

1 small **red onion**, finely chopped

3 tablespoons chopped **coriander leaves**

1 tablespoon **mint**, chopped

4 tablespoons **lemon juice**

salt and **pepper**

12 **filo pastry** sheets, each about 30 x 18 cm (12 x 7 inches)

melted **butter**, for brushing

500 g (1 lb) **chicken breast**, cut into 2.5 cm (1 inch) x 5 cm (2 inch) slices

ready-made satay sauce, to serve

Marinade:

1 tablespoon **ground cinnamon**

1 tablespoon **ground cumin**

1 teaspoon **pepper**

150 ml (¼ pint) **vegetable oil**

100 ml (3½ fl oz) **soy sauce**

2 tablespoons **light brown sugar**

To garnish:

raw **onion**, chopped

cucumber chunks, roughly chopped

PREP

10*

COOK

10

SERVES

4

share

cool

saucy

chicken satay

This classic, nutty Indonesian dish can also be cooked with lamb, beef or pork instead of chicken, if you like. You will need bamboo or metal skewers to make this recipe.

1 Put the chicken slices in a bowl and add all the ingredients for the marinade. Stir well and make sure that all the chicken pieces are covered in the marinade. Leave for at least 4 hours, but preferably overnight. Give the chicken an occasional stir.

2 Carefully spear the chicken pieces onto the skewers, leaving some space at either end. Put them under a hot grill for about 2 minutes, turning once. As you cannot see if the chicken is cooked through, test one piece – you can always grill it for a little longer if you need to.

3 You will have to cook the skewers in batches, so keep the cooked chicken warm while waiting for them all to be done.

4 Put on top of raw onion and cucumber and dip into the satay sauce.

*Plus 4 hours marinating

garlic and herb mushrooms

PREP

10

COOK

5

SERVES

4

posh

party

yum!

These taste so gloriously garlicky, and are surprisingly 'meaty', too. Have as a starter before a pizza for an authentic Italian meal.

1 Heat the oil in a large frying pan. Fry the mushrooms over a high heat, turning once, until they start to colour.

2 Add the garlic and fry for 1–2 minutes. Splash on the lemon juice and parsley, stir to mix well, then sprinkle with salt and pepper.

3 Put the mushrooms on four plates and pour the juices from the pan over them. Top with shavings of Parmesan and eat straight away with a salad or some crusty bread.

3 tablespoons **olive oil**

12 large **mushrooms**

2 **garlic cloves**, thinly sliced

2 tablespoons **lemon juice**

3 tablespoons **parsley**, finely chopped

salt and **pepper**

Parmesan cheese, shaved

fast food

250 g (8 oz) small **new potatoes**, scrubbed, **or medium potatoes**, scrubbed and quartered

200 g (7 oz) **can tuna**, drained and roughly flaked

5 tablespoons **olive oil**

2 tablespoons **red wine vinegar**

salt and **pepper**

1 **red pepper**

250 g (8 oz) **green beans,** cut into 5 cm (2 inch) lengths

2 **garlic cloves**, finely chopped

2 **anchovy fillets**, chopped

½–1 teaspoon **mustard**

2 tablespoons **capers**

PREP

10

COOK

15

SERVES

2

posh

fresh

yum!

salade niçoise

It is impossible to give a definitive recipe for Salade Niçoise as there is a lot of controversy over what should be included – so why not experiment and make up your own version.

1 Boil the potatoes for 8–10 minutes, until just tender. Put in a large bowl, add the tuna and toss gently with 1 tablespoon each of the oil and vinegar and sprinkle with some salt and pepper.

2 Meanwhile, place the red pepper under a hot grill and cook for about 10 minutes, turning as necessary, until the skin is black and blistered. Transfer the pepper to a plastic bag until cool then peel off the skin. Core and deseed the pepper and cut it into thin slices.

3 Boil the green beans for 5–6 minutes until just tender and still a bit crunchy. Drain and put on one side.

4 Add the rest of the oil to the frying pan, then stir in the garlic and anchovies and fry for 30 seconds. Stir in the rest of the vinegar and boil for about 1 minute. Stir in the mustard, then pour over the potato mixture. Add the pepper strips, beans, capers and more pepper. Toss gently, taste and add more salt and pepper if you want, then eat straight away while warm and juicy.

caesar salad

It's incredible that a few really ordinary ingredients can taste so good! Experiment by adding bacon, tuna or strips of chicken and you will never get bored of it.

1 Put the garlic, anchovies, lemon juice, mustard and egg yolk in a small bowl and sprinkle with pepper. Mix well until combined. Slowly drizzle in the olive oil, mixing all the time to make a thick creamy sauce. If the sauce is too thick, add a little water.

2 Heat the vegetable oil in a frying pan. Test with a small piece of bread to see if it is hot enough; if the bread sizzles add the rest of the bread, turning them when they are golden brown, then drain on kitchen paper.

3 Put the lettuce into a large bowl, pour over the dressing and 2 tablespoons of the Parmesan cheese and mix well. Sprinkle on the croûtons and the rest of the Parmesan and it's ready to eat.

share

fab

fast

1 **garlic clove**, peeled and crushed

4 **anchovy fillets**, chopped

juice of 1 **lemon**

1–2 teaspoons **mustard**

1 **egg yolk**

pepper

200 ml (7 fl oz) **olive oil**

vegetable oil for frying

3 slices white **bread**, cut into cubes

1 **Cos lettuce**, washed and torn into pieces

3 tablespoons **Parmesan cheese**, grated

1 ripe **avocado**, halved, peeled and stone removed

2 tablespoons **lemon juice**

500 g (1 lb) young **spinach leaves**

1 small bunch **spring onions**, shredded into long, thin strips

2 tablespoons **vegetable oil**

4 rashers **rindless back bacon**, chopped

1 **garlic clove**, crushed

Dressing:

3 tablespoons **balsamic vinegar**

1 teaspoon **soft light brown sugar**

1 teaspoon **Dijon mustard**

salt and **pepper**

125 ml (4 fl oz) **olive oil**

1 tablespoon **finely chopped walnuts**

1 tablespoon chopped **parsley or basil**

PREP

 15

COOK

 10

SERVES

4

 posh

 fresh

 fab

spinach, avocado and bacon salad

The secret of this yummy salad is to serve it quickly while the bacon is still warm and the salad leaves still look and taste fresh.

1 First make the dressing. Mix the vinegar, sugar and mustard in a bowl. Add a dash of salt and pepper, then slowly whisk in the olive oil. Stir the chopped walnuts and herbs into the dressing and add more salt and pepper if needed.

2 Chop the avocado into cubes and sprinkle with lemon juice to stop it from going brown.

3 Tear the spinach leaves into pieces and put in a bowl together with the spring onion strips and avocado cubes.

4 Fry the bacon and the garlic until crisp and brown, then drain on kitchen paper. Scatter over the spinach mixture.

5 Drizzle some of the dressing over the salad, toss gently and eat straight away.

tuna pasta salad

One of the very best pasta salads – perfect for a picnic. The combination of tuna, walnuts and pesto also makes a very good hot sauce with pasta.

1 Cook the pasta according to the packet instructions, then drain. Plunge under cold water to stop it from cooking more, and drain again. Put in a bowl.

2 Mix the pesto sauce and vinegar in a bowl and sprinkle with pepper. Add to the pasta with the grated lemon rind and toss.

3 Mix the tuna and walnuts into the pasta. Sprinkle over the basil and drizzle the olive oil over the top. Mix and eat immediately.

PREP

COOK

SERVES

400 g (13 oz) **pasta shells**

5 tablespoons **pesto**

1 teaspoon **white wine vinegar**

pepper

1 teaspoon grated **lemon rind**

200 g (7 oz) **can tuna**, drained and flaked

50 g (2 oz) **chopped walnut pieces**

6 large **basil leaves**, shredded

3 tablespoons **olive oil**

1 unpeeled **dessert apple**, cored and cut into small squares

2 **carrots**, about 250 g (8 oz), grated

2 tablespoons finely chopped **gherkins**

2 teaspoons **capers**

2 tablespoons chopped **parsley**

¼–½ **white cabbage** or **cabbage heart**, finely shredded

Spiced dressing:

3 tablespoons **mayonnaise**

½ teaspoon **curry powder**

½ teaspoon **ground nutmeg**

½ teaspoon **paprika**

½–1 teaspoon **mustard**

1 tablespoon **olive oil**

1 tablespoon **lemon juice**

salt and **pepper**

PREP

15

COOK

SERVES

4

cheap

easy

spicy

spicy coleslaw

This is a lively version of this traditional salad, which is delicious with chicken or fish.

1 Make the dressing by whisking all the ingredients together.

2 Add the apple and carrots to the dressing, together with the gherkins, capers and parsley. Mix well, then add the cabbage and mix again.

guacamole

PREP

10

This thick, creamy avocado dip from Mexico is great with tortillas or, for a tasty and healthy snack, simply dip in celery, cucumber or carrots.

COOK

SERVES

4

1 Put the avocado into a bowl with the lime or lemon juice and mash to make a textured but not smooth paste.

2 Stir in the garlic, onion, tomato, chillies, coriander and sugar. Sprinkle with salt and pepper and add some extra lime or lemon juice if you want. Eat straight away.

posh

yum!

snack

2 large ripe **avocados**, halved, peeled and stone removed

juice of 1 **lime or lemon**

1 **garlic clove**, crushed

1 tablespoon **onion**, finely chopped

1 large **tomato**, skinned, deseeded and finely chopped

1–2 **fresh green chillies**, deseeded and finely chopped

1 tablespoon **coriander leaves**, finely chopped

pinch of **sugar**

salt and **pepper**

paprika potato wedges

4 large **baking potatoes**, unpeeled

4 tablespoons **vegetable oil**

1–2 teaspoons **paprika**

salt

soured cream mixed with **chives**, or **mayonnaise**, to dip into

PREP

5

COOK

40

SERVES

4

mates

fab

beer

These are fab for a party, and are great with a really cold beer or glass of wine. Have a couple of little dishes with dips such as soured cream, ketchup or garlic mayo and your guests will be happy.

1 Heat the oven to 220°C (425°F), Gas Mark 7.

2 Scrub the potatoes, rinse and pat dry. Cut each potato lengthways into 8 wedges.

3 Put the wedges in a roasting tin, drizzle over the oil and toss well to coat the potatoes. Sprinkle with the paprika and salt.

4 Roast the potatoes for 35–40 minutes, spooning the oil over them 2–3 times. Then sprinkle with salt and dig in.

potato skins with soured cream

Another ace party food. You can also sprinkle bacon bits over the top, or add chopped herbs for a bit of colour.

PREP

15

COOK

90

MAKES

20

telly

party

yum!

5 large **baking potatoes**, unpeeled

150 ml (¼ pint) **soured cream**

1 teaspoon **chives**, chopped

salt and **pepper**

vegetable oil, for brushing

1 Heat the oven to 190°C (375°F), Gas Mark 5.

2 Scrub the potatoes, rinse and pat dry. Prick the potatoes then bake in the oven for about 1¼ hours until tender.

3 Meanwhile, make the dip. Mix the soured cream with the chives and a good dash of salt and pepper and chill.

4 Leave the potatoes to cool for a few minutes, then cut each one in half lengthways and then again to make 4 long pieces. Using a teaspoon, scoop out most of the potato, leaving just a thin layer next to the skin.

5 Brush the potato skins with oil, then fry over a medium heat for 5–7 minutes on each side until golden. Sprinkle with salt and dip into the soured cream.

1 large **baking potato**, unpeeled

½ large **parsnip**, about 150 g (5 oz)

2 **carrots**, about 250 g (8 oz)

3 tablespoons **olive oil**

pinch of **turmeric**

pinch of **paprika**

2 **eggs**

baked egg and chips

This is a fab fuss-free oven-baked version of egg and chips.

1 Heat the oven to 220°C (425°F), Gas Mark 7.

2 Scrub the potato and peel the parsnip and carrots. Cut the potato and parsnip into wedges and the carrots into sticks, all about 6 cm (2½ inches) long.

3 Boil the vegetables for 4 minutes then drain. Meanwhile, heat the oil in a small roasting tin in the oven for 2 minutes.

4 Sprinkle the spices over the vegetables, toss them in the oil so they are well covered and roast in the oven for 20 minutes. Turn the vegetables and make a hole in the middle of them. Break the eggs into the hole and bake for another 5 minutes until well cooked. Then dish up with ketchup.

breakfast gratin

This is a great vegetarian alternative to the traditional British fry-up. Ideal if you are suffering from the excesses of the night before.

PREP

15

COOK

20

SERVES

2

1 Heat half the oil in a large frying pan over a medium heat, add the mushrooms and onion and fry for 5 minutes until golden, then put on a plate. Add the rest of the oil and fry the potatoes for 5–6 minutes until golden.

2 Turn up the heat, add the tomatoes and fry for 2–3 minutes, then put the mushrooms and onions back in the pan.

3 Make 4 holes in the mixture and break an egg into each one. Sprinkle over the cheese then put the pan under a hot grill for 4–5 minutes until the eggs are set and the cheese is bubbling.

4 Sprinkle with salt and pepper and chives or parsley, then eat with hot buttered toast.

mates

fab

yum!

4 tablespoons **vegetable oil**

175 g (6 oz) **button mushrooms**, quartered if large

1 **onion**, roughly chopped

4 small **potatoes**, cooked, peeled and chopped into cubes

4 small **tomatoes**, halved

4 **eggs**

125 g (4 oz) **Cheddar cheese**, grated

salt and **pepper**

2 tablespoons **chives or parsley**, chopped

4 ripe **tomatoes**, halved

2 tablespoons chopped **basil**

4 tablespoons **vegetable oil**

salt and **pepper**

4 slices **ham**

1 tablespoon **vinegar**

4 large **eggs**

toast or toasted muffins, to serve

poached eggs with ham and herb tomatoes

This delicious combination is the healthy version of a traditional greasy full English.

1 Put the tomatoes cut-side up on a grill pan. Mix the basil with 2 tablespoons of the oil and drizzle over the cut tomatoes. Add lots of salt and pepper. Cook under a medium grill for about 6–7 minutes, until soft.

2 Meanwhile, heat the rest of the oil in a frying pan and fry the ham until crisp. Drain on kitchen paper.

3 To poach the eggs, bring a large saucepan of water to the boil, add the vinegar, then stir the water rapidly in a circular motion to make a whirlpool. Break an egg into the centre of the pan and cook for 3 minutes. Dish up on buttered toasted muffins or toast with a slice of ham and some grilled tomatoes. Cook and serve the other 3 eggs in the same way.

onion rings in beer batter

These home-made onion rings are much superior to the frozen ones you can buy – maybe it's because of the beer!

PREP

10

COOK

10

SERVES

4

party

mates

boozy

4 large **onions**

vegetable oil, for deep-frying

Batter:

1 **egg**, separated

1 tablespoon **olive oil**

100 ml (3½ fl oz) **light beer**

65 g (2½ oz) **plain flour**

salt and **pepper**

1 Slice the onions into 5 mm (¼ inch) thick rings and separate out. Keep the larger rings and ditch the rest, or keep to fry up the next day for breakfast.

2 In a bowl, make the batter by beating together the egg yolk, oil, beer and flour and sprinkling with salt and pepper.

3 In another bowl whisk the egg white until stiff then mix into the batter until smooth.

4 Heat 5 cm (2 inches) of vegetable oil in a deep saucepan until really hot – you can test this by dropping in a cube of bread, which should cook in 30 seconds. Dip the onion rings, a few at a time, into the batter and then drop into the oil and deep-fry for 1–2 minutes until golden. Remove really carefully and drain on kitchen paper, then eat while hot with mayonnaise.

4 large **tomatoes**

2 tablespoons **vegetable oil**

1 **onion**, chopped

2 **garlic cloves**, crushed

2 **large green chillies**, jalapeño if you can get them, deseeded and chopped

pinch of **dried oregano**

pinch of **ground cumin**

salt and **pepper**

250 g (8 oz) **tortilla chips**

125 g (4 oz) grated **Cheddar cheese**

To garnish:

2 **spring onions**, cut into strips

1 **red chilli**, deseeded and cut into strips

PREP

COOK

SERVES

share

spicy

mates

spicy nachos with cheese

Nachos are a really great party food – everyone loves them.

1 Heat the oven to 180°C (350°F), Gas Mark 4.

2 Cut a cross at the stem end of each tomato. Place the tomatoes in a bowl and pour boiling water over to cover. Leave for 1–2 minutes, then drain and peel off the skins. Cut the tomatoes into quarters, remove the seeds, and cut into strips.

3 Heat the oil in a saucepan and fry the onion and garlic until soft, giving them the occasional stir.

4 Add the tomatoes, chillies, oregano, cumin and a dash of salt and pepper. Bring to the boil, turn down the heat and simmer gently for 15 minutes, or until the chilli sauce is nice and thick.

5 Put the tortilla chips on a large ovenproof plate or dish and then dollop the chilli sauce over the top. Sprinkle with Cheddar cheese and cook in the oven for 10–15 minutes, or until the cheese melts and starts to bubble.

6 Sprinkle the spring onion and red chilli over the top of the nachos and enjoy!

great steak sandwich

This is a real treat – juicy steak with a hint of mustard and pepper. What more could you want when you're really hungry.

1 Heat 4 tablespoons of the oil in a medium frying pan. Add the onions and garlic, cover and cook over a very low heat for 30 minutes, until very soft but not coloured.

2 Put the onion mixture in a bowl, add the mustard and mash it up. Stir in the parsley and vinegar, and add a dash of salt and pepper. Cover and put to one side.

3 Brush the steaks with a little of the rest of the oil. Press the crushed black peppercorns into both sides. Put the steaks under a medium hot grill and cook to taste: for 4–5 minutes on each side for medium-rare, or 5–6 minutes for medium.

4 Toast the bread on both sides. Spread 4 slices with the onion purée and cover with slices of tomato. Add a piece of steak to each and top with the cheese slices and rocket. Sprinkle with salt and pepper, cover with the rest of the toast, and dig in while it's hot.

PREP

20

COOK

40

SERVES

4

sexy

cool

telly

5 tablespoons **olive oil**

2 large **red onions**, thinly sliced

2 **garlic cloves**, crushed

1 teaspoon **mustard**

1 tablespoon **parsley**, chopped

1 tablespoon **balsamic vinegar**

salt and **pepper**

4 x 125–150 g (4–5 oz) **sirloin steaks**

1 tablespoon **black peppercorns**, crushed

8 large slices of crusty **bread**

2 large **tomatoes**, sliced

75 g (3 oz) **Gruyère cheese**, thinly sliced

125 g (4 oz) **rocket**

2 small skinless **chicken breasts**

1 **celery stick**

4 **spring onions**

10 cm (4 inch) length of **cucumber**

1 **carrot**, about 125 g (4 oz)

4 tablespoons **hoisin sauce**

2 large **wheat tortillas**

2 tablespoons **sesame seeds**

posh

fresh

yum!

chinese chicken wraps

Mexican influences and Chinese inspiration combine to make this delicious, innovative international sandwich.

1 Thinly slice the chicken breasts and cook under a medium grill for 3–4 minutes on each side until cooked through.

2 Cut the celery, spring onions and cucumber into 5 cm (2 inch) lengths, then cut them lengthways into fine shreds. Grate the carrot.

3 Spread the hoisin sauce over the tortillas to within 2.5 cm (1 inch) of the edge. Arrange the slices of chicken down the centre and sprinkle with the sesame seeds and shredded vegetables. Roll up the tortillas to enclose the filling and eat.

spanish tortilla

An authentic Spanish tortilla is traditionally made with just eggs, potatoes, onions, salt and pepper, but this version contains sliced red and green peppers for a bit of extra colour and flavour.

1 Heat all but 2 tablespoons of the oil in a large frying pan. Add the potato slices, onion and red and green peppers and cook, stirring lots, for 15 minutes, until all the vegetables are golden and tender.

2 In a bowl beat the eggs then stir in the potato mixture from the pan and add a dash of salt and pepper. Put on one side to stand for 15 minutes.

3 Heat the rest of the oil in the frying pan and tip in the tortilla mixture. Cook over a low heat for 10 minutes, until almost cooked through. Flip over and cook the other side for another 5 minutes, or until the tortilla is cooked on both sides. Leave it to cool then cut into wedges.

*Plus 15 minutes resting time

PREP

10*

COOK

30

SERVES
4

cheap

fab

fast

150 ml (¼ pint) **olive oil**

750 g (1½ lb) **potatoes**, thinly sliced

1 large **onion**, sliced

1 **red pepper**, cored, deseeded and sliced

1 **green pepper**, cored, deseeded and sliced

5 large **eggs**

salt and **pepper**

1 tablespoon **olive oil**

1 **onion**, finely chopped

200 g (7 oz) **pasta**

400 g (13 oz) **jar red peppers**, drained and cut into cubes

5 pieces **sun-dried tomatoes**, drained and thinly sliced

1–2 **garlic cloves**, crushed

400 g (13 oz) **can chopped tomatoes**

150 ml (¼ pint) **vegetable or chicken stock**

2 teaspoons **sugar**

salt and **pepper**

3 tablespoons **cream**

Parmesan cheese, grated, and **basil**, to serve

pasta with creamy red pepper sauce

Serve with salad and you have a simple but luxuriously tasty dinner in an instant.

1 Heat the oil in a small saucepan, add the onion and fry for 5 minutes, stirring occasionally, until pale golden.

2 Meanwhile, cook the pasta according to the packet instructions.

3 Add the peppers, sun-dried tomatoes and garlic to the onion. Fry for 2 more minutes, then add the canned tomatoes, stock, sugar and a dash of salt and pepper. Cook gently for 10 minutes, stirring from time to time.

4 Drain the pasta, then stir in the tomato sauce and cream. Toss together, then top with Parmesan cheese and basil leaves.

quick pasta carbonara

Easy and no fuss – you will have no problems with this creamy pasta!

1 Cook the pasta according to the packet instructions.

2 Meanwhile, heat the oil in a large frying pan. Add the onion and fry until soft. Then add the bacon or pancetta and garlic, and fry gently for 4–5 minutes.

3 Beat the eggs with the Parmesan cheese, parsley and cream. Sprinkle with salt and pepper and mix.

4 Drain the pasta and add it to the pan with the onion and bacon or pancetta. Stir over a gentle heat until well mixed, then pour in the egg mixture. Stir and take the pan off the heat. Carry on mixing well for a few seconds, until the eggs are lightly cooked and creamy, then eat with a green salad.

PREP

10

COOK

10

SERVES

4

sexy

snack

fast

400 g (13 oz) **spaghetti** or other long thin pasta

2 tablespoons **olive oil**

1 **onion**, finely chopped

200 g (7 oz) **rindless bacon or pancetta**, cut into cubes

2 **garlic cloves**, finely chopped

3 **eggs**

4 tablespoons grated **Parmesan cheese**

3 tablespoons chopped **parsley**

3 tablespoons **cream**

salt and **pepper**

cheat's calzone

2 small **wheat tortillas**

2 teaspoons **sun-dried tomato paste**

1 **tomato**, sliced

75 g (3 oz) **mozzarella cheese**, thinly sliced

few **basil leaves**, plus extra to top

4–6 **spinach leaves**

1 tablespoon **olive oil**

salt and **pepper**

Traditionally, calzone is made with a soft pizza dough which is folded to encase the filling. This is a bit of cheat, but it's so much easier to just use a tortilla that who cares?

1 Rinse the tortillas with water to soften them, so they will fold and stick together. Dollop tomato paste over half of each tortilla and then chuck the tomato and mozzarella on top. Add the basil leaves and spinach and a dash of salt and pepper.

2 Fold each tortilla over the filling and press the edges together (don't worry if the edges don't stick together in places). Heat the oil in a frying pan, add the tortillas and fry for 1–2 minutes on each side, until golden, then dish up immediately.

posh

fast

Other fillings:

Try a filling of grated or sliced Cheddar cheese, chopped ham and mushrooms or your own favourite pizza combo.

Use a little pesto instead of the basil leaves and frozen spinach instead of fresh (but defrost it first and drain well).

easy

sticky barbecued ribs

This sauce is so sexily tangy and gooey that it also works equally well with chops or chicken breasts.

1 Heat the oven to 200°C (400°F), Gas Mark 6.

2 Put the ribs in a roasting tin.

3 Mix the ketchup, sugar, oil, Worcestershire sauce and mustard together in a bowl. Pour the mixture over the ribs and make sure they are all well covered, then pour the stock over the top.

4 Roast in the oven for 1¼ hours, basting the ribs once or twice with the juices and turning the very brown ribs over so they don't burn. Serve with salad.

PREP

10

COOK

75

SERVES

2

gooey

fun

saucy

1.25 kg (2½ lb) **pork ribs**

5 tablespoons **tomato ketchup**

3 tablespoons **brown sugar**

2 tablespoons **vegetable oil**

2 tablespoons **Worcestershire sauce**

1–2 teaspoons **mustard**

450 ml (¾ pint) **chicken stock**

veggie feasts

375 g (12 oz) **pasta**

1 tablespoon **vegetable oil**

1 **garlic clove**, crushed

1 **onion**, sliced

½ teaspoon **dried chilli flakes**

700 g (1 lb 6 oz) **passata**

225 g (7½ oz) **spinach leaves**

150 g (5 oz) **ricotta cheese**

salt and **pepper**

easy

posh

yum!

pasta with tomato, ricotta and spinach

This is a gloriously simple dish. All you need is some chunky bread so you can mop up every last bit of the sauce.

1 Cook the pasta according to the packet instructions and drain.

2 Meanwhile, heat the oil in a large saucepan, toss in the garlic and onion and fry gently for 3–4 minutes, then add the chilli flakes and fry for 1 minute.

3 Stir in the passata and let it simmer for 2 minutes. Add the spinach and ricotta, stir until the spinach has wilted, then simmer for 3–4 minutes.

4 Toss the pasta through the sauce, sprinkle with salt and pepper and eat immediately.

penne with spicy tomatoes

A filling pasta dish with a spicy kick. Peeling the tomatoes might seem a bit fiddly, but it's well worth it for the flavour.

1 Cut a cross at the stem end of each tomato. Put the tomatoes in a bowl and pour boiling water over to cover. Leave for 1–2 minutes, then drain and peel off the skins. Cut the tomatoes into quarters, remove the seeds, and cut into strips.

2 Cook the pasta according to the packet instructions.

3 Meanwhile, heat the vegetable oil in a saucepan, then gently fry the onion and garlic until soft; do not let them brown. Add the dried chilli.

4 Add the tomatoes to the onion mixture. Over a low heat, add the sugar, vinegar and salt and pepper then simmer for 5 minutes.

5 Drain the pasta. Stir the parsley into the tomato sauce, then mix the sauce in with the pasta, add a dash of olive oil and sprinkle with Parmesan. Lovely!

PREP

10

COOK

20

SERVES

4

fast

spicy

mates

10 large **tomatoes**

375 g (12 oz) **penne pasta**

3 tablespoons **vegetable oil**

1 **onion**, chopped

2 **garlic cloves**, crushed

2 pinches **dried chilli flakes**

1 teaspoon **sugar**

1 teaspoon **vinegar**

salt and **pepper**

handful of **parsley**, chopped

olive oil, for drizzling

75 g (3 oz) **Parmesan cheese**, grated

1 kg (2 lb) **tomatoes or** 2 x 400 g (13 oz) **cans chopped tomatoes**

2 tablespoons **olive oil**

2 **onions**, finely chopped

2 **garlic cloves**, crushed

1 tablespoon **balsamic or red wine vinegar**

salt and **pepper**

375 g (12 oz) **spaghetti**

Parmesan or Cheddar cheese, grated, to serve

10

15

spaghetti with tomato sauce

Pasta is so cheap, convenient and comforting, and this rich and versatile tomato sauce suits most tastes. For a different flavour chuck in some capers, black olives, fresh basil, parsley and oregano or anchovies.

SERVES

4

fast

yum!

cheap

1 If using fresh tomatoes, cut a cross at the stem end of each one. Put in a bowl and pour boiling water over to cover. Leave them for 1–2 minutes, then drain, peel off the skins and cut into quarters.

2 Heat the oil in a saucepan or frying pan, and fry the onions for 3–4 minutes until soft. Add the garlic and fry for 1 minute.

3 Stir in the tomatoes, vinegar and a dash of salt and pepper. Cook over a medium heat, stirring frequently, for about 10 minutes until the tomatoes are soft and pulpy. If the mixture gets too dry, just add a little water.

4 Meanwhile, cook the pasta according to the packet instructions. Drain, and add the tomato sauce. Toss lightly then dish up straight away, sprinkling Parmesan or Cheddar cheese over the top.

spaghetti with olive oil and garlic

This is a great recipe for when there's no food in your cupboard as all it needs is a few basic ingredients.

PREP

5

COOK

10

SERVES

4

375 g (12 oz) **spaghetti**

5 tablespoons **extra virgin olive oil**

2 **garlic cloves**, chopped

1–2 **dried red chillies**, finely chopped

salt and **pepper**

1 Cook the spaghetti according to the packet instructions, then drain.

2 Pour the oil into the empty pasta pan and gently fry the garlic and chillies. Keep stirring until they start to sizzle. Sprinkle on some salt and pepper.

3 Tip the pasta back into the pan and stir it all up so that the spaghetti is coated in oil. Dish it up and enjoy!

cool

easy

posh

375 g (12 oz) **spaghetti**

½ tablespoon **vegetable oil**

1 **onion**, chopped

200 g (7 oz) **can baby carrots**, drained and chopped

1 **leek**, sliced

2 **celery sticks**, sliced

400 g (13 oz) **can chopped tomatoes**

1 tablespoon **tomato purée**

1 teaspoon **cayenne pepper**

125 g (4 oz) **mushrooms**, sliced

salt and **pepper**

PREP

15

COOK

10

SERVES

4

cheap

easy

mates

vegetable bolognese

This tasty meat-free Bolognese sauce is worth making in bulk and then freezing as it makes an instant tasty meal served with rice, pasta or potatoes.

1 Cook the pasta according to the packet instructions.

2 Meanwhile, heat the oil in a saucepan. Add the onion and fry over a low heat for 3–5 minutes, until soft. Stir in the carrots, leek and celery, then the tomatoes, tomato purée, cayenne and mushrooms. Add a pinch of salt and pepper and simmer for 10 minutes.

3 Drain the pasta and sprinkle with pepper. To serve, mound up the spaghetti and dollop the Bolognese over the top.

cheesy spinach lasagne

This is a great meal to cook when friends come over. Lasagne is always a winner when you dish it up with garlic bread and salad.

1 Put the spinach into a large saucepan with just the water that clings to the leaves, cover the pan and cook over a high heat for 1–2 minutes until wilted. Drain thoroughly, then chop finely.

2 Heat the oven to 190°C (375°F), Gas Mark 5.

3 Heat the oil, add the onions and garlic and fry until soft. Mix with the spinach.

4 Make the cheese sauce: heat the butter or margarine in a saucepan, stir in the flour, then slowly add the milk. Bring to the boil, then stir or whisk into a smooth sauce. Stir most of both cheeses, the mustard, and a dash of salt and pepper into the sauce.

5 Arrange the lasagne, sauce and spinach in layers in a 1.8 litre (3 pint) ovenproof dish, starting with one-third of the lasagne and ending with lasagne and sauce.

6 Sprinkle the rest of the Cheddar and Parmesan over the top and bake for 25–30 minutes in the oven, then dish up with a mixed salad and garlic bread.

PREP

40

COOK

25

SERVES

4

posh

share

fun

500 g–750 g (1–1½ lb) **fresh spinach**, washed

salt and **pepper**

1½ tablespoons **vegetable oil**

2 **onions**, finely chopped

2 **garlic cloves**, finely chopped

9 sheets ready-to-cook **lasagne**

Cheese sauce:

50 g (2 oz) **butter or margarine**

50 g (2 oz) **flour**

750 ml (1¼ pints) **milk**

175 g (6 oz) **Cheddar cheese**, grated

2–3 tablespoons **Parmesan cheese**, grated

1 teaspoon **mustard**

salt and **pepper**

10 ready-to-cook **cannelloni tubes**

Filling:

375 g (12 oz) **ricotta cheese**

250 g (8 oz) **fresh spinach**, cooked, drained and chopped

1 **egg**, beaten

25 g (1 oz) **plain flour**

2 tablespoons **garlic purée**

salt and **pepper**

Sauce and topping:

1 tablespoon **vegetable oil**

1 **onion**, chopped

550 g (18 oz) **passata**

2 teaspoons **dried mixed herbs**

250 g (8 oz) **mozzarella cheese**, grated

share

yum!

cool

spinach cannelloni

All you really need to go with this is a good bottle of red wine …

1 Heat the oven to 190°C (375°F), Gas Mark 5.

2 Make the filling by mixing all the ingredients together.

3 Make the sauce by heating the oil in a pan and frying the onion until soft. Stir in the passata and herbs and simmer for 5 minutes.

4 Fill each cannelloni tube with some of the filling.

5 Put the tubes in a greased 1.8 litre (3 pint) or similar ovenproof dish. Pour over the sauce and top with the grated mozzarella. Bake for 45 minutes then enjoy!

mushroom risotto

Try to get two or three different types of mushrooms – even splash out and buy some wild mushrooms – and you will create a really delicious meal.

1 Melt the butter in a large saucepan. Add the onion and garlic and fry gently for 5 minutes, until soft, but not coloured. Stir in the mushrooms and herbs, and cook over a medium heat for 3 minutes. Glug in the wine, bring to the boil and cook, stirring, until almost all the liquid has evaporated.

2 Add the rice and stir well so it is covered in the butter. Add the stock, a bit at a time, stirring until each glug is absorbed into the rice. Continue adding the stock, cooking until the rice is creamy but still firm, which should take about 20 minutes. Taste it and add salt and pepper if needed.

3 Cover the pan and leave the risotto to rest for a few minutes, scatter some grated Parmesan over the top and enjoy with the rest of the bottle of wine!

PREP

COOK

30

SERVES

6

posh

fab

party

125 g (4 oz) **butter**

1 large **onion**, finely chopped

2 **garlic cloves**, finely chopped

175 g (6 oz) **mushrooms**, roughly chopped (use different kinds if you can)

2 teaspoons **thyme**, chopped

2 teaspoons **marjoram**, chopped

150 ml (¼ pint) **white wine**

500 g (1 lb) **risotto rice**

1.5 litres (2½ pints) hot **chicken** or **vegetable stock**

salt and **pepper**

75 g (3 oz) **Parmesan cheese**, grated

4 **ready-to-cook pizza bases**

olive oil, for brushing

2 **onions**, finely sliced

2 **garlic cloves**, crushed and chopped

250 g (8 oz) **mushrooms**, sliced

salt and **pepper**

handful of **parsley**, chopped, **or chilli oil**, to serve

fun

party

yum!

mushroom pizzas

Sometimes the simple things are the best, and this yummy pizza really doesn't need anything else added to it. It's worth buying a few different kinds of mushroom to jazz this up.

1 Heat the oven to 230°C (450°F), Gas Mark 8.

2 Put the pizza bases onto baking sheets and brush lightly with olive oil.

3 Mix together the onions, garlic and mushrooms and a dash of salt and pepper. Spread the mixture over the pizzas and bake for 10–15 minutes.

4 Sprinkle the pizzas with parsley, or add a glug of chilli oil, and enjoy.

fresh vegetable pizzas

These are topped with so many nutritious vegetables you can almost convince yourself that these pizzas are actually good for you!

1 Heat the oven to 230°C (450°F), Gas Mark 8.

2 Put the pizza bases onto baking sheets, brush with a little olive oil, then chuck the garlic, vegetables and basil randomly on top.

3 Sprinkle over lots of salt and pepper and add a glug of olive oil, then bake for 10 minutes. The vegetables should be slightly charred (but not burnt!) around the edges. Shave some Parmesan over the top and you have the perfect lunch.

PREP

30

COOK

10

SERVES

4

mates

easy

share

4 **ready-to-cook pizza bases**

5 tablespoons **olive oil**

2 **garlic cloves**, chopped

1 **red onion**, finely sliced

2 **courgettes**, thinly sliced lengthways

1 **red pepper**, cored, deseeded and cut into thin strips

1 **yellow pepper**, cored, deseeded and cut into thin strips

4 large **tomatoes**, skinned and cut into small wedges

425 g (14 oz) **can sweetcorn**

handful of **basil leaves**, roughly torn

salt and **pepper**

75 g (3 oz) **Parmesan cheese**

2 tablespoons **vegetable oil**

1 **onion**, finely chopped

1 teaspoon **cumin**

½ teaspoon **cayenne pepper**

½ teaspoon **ground cinnamon**

2 **garlic cloves**, crushed

2 small **carrots**, chopped

1 **courgette**, thickly sliced

200 g (7 oz) **can chickpeas**, drained and rinsed

1 **red pepper**, cored, deseeded and cut into cubes

50 g (2 oz) ready-to-eat **dried apricots**, chopped

500 ml (17 fl oz) boiling **vegetable stock**

400 ml (14 fl oz) **water**

250 g (8 oz) **couscous**

4 tablespoons chopped **coriander leaves**

salt and **pepper**

PREP

COOK

SERVES

fab

posh

spicy

spiced vegetable couscous

Couscous comes from North Africa and is wonderfully easy, cheap and versatile. Don't panic if you don't have all the ingredients, as this is a dish to experiment with. As long as you have the staples you can chuck in anything else that you think will work.

1 Heat the oil in a large frying pan. Add the onion and fry gently for 3–4 minutes until soft but not brown.

2 Stir in the cumin, cayenne, cinnamon and garlic. Cook, stirring, for 1 minute. Stir in the carrots, courgette, chickpeas, red pepper and apricots and cook for 2–3 minutes.

3 Pour in the boiling stock and bring back to the boil. Turn down the heat, cover the pan and simmer gently for 8–10 minutes.

4 Meanwhile, boil the water in a saucepan. Add the couscous, stir, and take off the heat.

5 Taste the vegetables and add salt and pepper if they need it, then stir in the coriander.

6 Stir up the couscous with a fork until it is light and fluffy and add a dash of salt and pepper. Dish up the couscous then pour the veggies and their sauce over the top of it all.

vegetables with couscous stuffing

Peppers and large tomatoes make excellent containers for savoury stuffings – use a mixture of peppers and tomatoes or just stick to one, depending on what you like.

PREP

15

COOK

30

SERVES
4

saucy

cool

fresh

2 large **tomatoes**

2 **red, orange or yellow peppers**

2 tablespoons **olive oil**

salt and **pepper**

300 ml (½ pint) **water**

175 g (6 oz) **couscous**

½ bunch of **spring onions**, trimmed and chopped

handful of **basil leaves**, roughly torn

125 g (4 oz) **mozzarella cheese**, drained and chopped

25 g (1 oz) **Parmesan cheese**, grated

400 g (13 oz) **can chickpeas**, drained and rinsed

1 Heat the oven to 200°C (400°F), Gas Mark 6.

2 Cut the tomatoes in half horizontally and scoop out the pulp and seeds. Halve the peppers lengthways and ditch the core and seeds. Put the tomatoes and peppers, cup-side up, in a large shallow ovenproof dish, drizzle with the oil and sprinkle with salt and pepper. Bake in the oven for 20 minutes until soft.

3 Meanwhile, boil the water in a saucepan. Add the couscous, stir, and take off the heat and leave for 10 minutes until the water has been absorbed. Fluff up the couscous with a fork and stir in the spring onions, basil, mozzarella, Parmesan, chickpeas and salt and pepper.

4 Spoon the couscous into the baked vegetables and bake in the oven for another 8–10 minutes until the mozzarella has melted. Eat while warm with salad and bread.

300 g (10 oz) **tofu**

175 g (6 oz) **egg noodles**

150 g (5 oz) **frozen peas**

2 tablespoons **vegetable oil**

1 bunch of **spring onions**, sliced

300 g (10 oz) **pack mixed stir-fry vegetables** (shredded cabbage, baby corn, beansprouts, peppers etc.)

150 ml (¼ pint) **hoisin sauce**

3 tablespoons **orange juice**

salt and **pepper**

fast

mates

fresh

chinese stir-fry noodles

If you want to jazz up this dish, try adding some cashew nuts or water chestnuts for a bit of extra crunch.

1 Drain the tofu, pat dry on kitchen paper and cut into small cubes.

2 Cook or soak the noodles following the packet instructions. Boil the frozen peas for 2 minutes then drain.

3 Heat the oil in a large frying pan or wok. Fry the spring onions and ready-prepared vegetables, stirring, for 3–4 minutes until soft. Add the tofu, peas, hoisin sauce and orange juice and stir for 1 minute.

4 Drain the noodles, add to the pan, toss everything together and add salt and pepper if it needs it. Tuck in straight away while it's hot and crunchy.

mixed vegetable stir-fry

This is one of those dishes where you really can chuck whatever veggies you have into the wok – the only slightly tricky part is making sure that they are cooked in the right order. So use this as a guide and experiment!

1 Heat the oil in a wok or large frying pan. Add the garlic and stir-fry quickly over a medium heat until golden but not too brown.

2 Stir in the cabbage, cauliflower, broccoli, and a good dash of pepper. Glug in the oyster sauce and stock, and then cook, stirring constantly, for 3 minutes.

3 Add the carrots, mushrooms, onion and bean sprouts and stir-fry for 2 minutes. Dish up straight away.

PREP

15

COOK

6

SERVES

4

easy

spicy

share

3 tablespoons **vegetable oil**

1 **garlic clove**, crushed

125 g (4 oz) **cabbage**, shredded

125 g (4 oz) **cauliflower**, divided into florets

125 g (4 oz) **broccoli**, divided into florets

pepper

2 tablespoons **oyster sauce**

150 ml (¼ pint) **chicken or vegetable stock**

2 small **carrots**, cut into thin strips

125 g (4 oz) **mushrooms**, thinly sliced

1 **onion**, sliced

50 g (2 oz) **bean sprouts**

300 g (10 oz) **tofu**

3 tablespoons **lemon juice**

3 **garlic cloves**, chopped

½ tablespoon **rosemary**, chopped

125 ml (4 fl oz) **olive oil**

400 g (13 oz) **aubergines**

salt and **pepper**

400 g (13 oz) **tomatoes**

250 g (8 oz) **courgettes**

8 **black olives**

125 ml (4 fl oz) **vegetable stock**

1 teaspoon **dried mixed herbs**

fresh

cheap

share

tofu ragout

Tofu is not only cheap and versatile, but is really good for you. Great to eat if you are feeling a bit run-down and are suffering from too many late nights.

1 Drain the tofu and cut into cubes. Mix the lemon juice with the garlic, rosemary and 2 tablespoons of the olive oil. Pour over the tofu, cover and leave for 2 hours.

2 Wash the aubergines, trim off the tops and bottoms and slice them lengthways. Sprinkle with salt and put on a plate.

3 Meanwhile, score the base of each tomato and put into boiling water for 30 seconds. Remove, then skin, cut in half, remove the seeds and chop roughly. Cut the courgettes into sticks.

4 Pat the aubergine dry with kitchen paper. Heat the rest of the oil in a large frying pan and fry the aubergines until golden brown, remove from the pan. Then fry the courgettes.

5 Put the aubergine slices into a saucepan and cover with the courgettes, tomatoes, olives and tofu. Add the stock, herbs and salt and pepper. Cover and cook over a medium heat for about 5 minutes, then dish up.

*Plus 2 hours' marinating

veggie lentil bake

The deliciously nutty lentils work really well in this hearty bake. Add some pickles, chutney and a salad and you have a great vegetarian main course.

PREP

10

COOK

70

SERVES

4

fab

mates

easy

1 Heat the oven to 200°C (400°F), Gas Mark 6.

2 Heat the oil in a saucepan, add the onion and fry for 4–5 minutes until slightly brown. Add the carrots, celery and garlic, cook for 1 minute, then stir in the lentils, stock and tomato purée. Bring to the boil and simmer uncovered, stirring now and then, for 30 minutes or until the lentils are soft. Sprinkle with salt and pepper.

3 Meanwhile, boil the potatoes for 15 minutes, until tender. Drain and mash with the milk, half the butter or margarine and a dash of salt and pepper.

4 Spoon the lentils into four 300 ml (½ pint) ovenproof dishes. Cover with the mashed potato.

5 Dot the rest of the butter on top and bake for 20 minutes until piping hot, then eat straight away.

1 tablespoon **vegetable oil**

1 **onion**, finely chopped

2 **carrots**, chopped

2 **celery sticks**, sliced

1 **garlic clove**, crushed

100 g (3½ oz) **red lentils**, rinsed

900 ml (1½ pints) **vegetable stock**

2 teaspoons **tomato purée**

salt and **pepper**

625 g (1¼ lb) **potatoes**, peeled and cut into chunks

3 tablespoons **milk**

40 g (1½ oz) **butter or margarine**

50 g (2 oz) **butter or margarine,** extra for greasing

2 large **onions,** finely chopped

125 g (4 oz) **cashew nuts or peanuts,** finely chopped

125 g (4 oz) **hazelnuts or almonds,** finely chopped

125 g (4 oz) **breadcrumbs**

1 teaspoon **dried mixed herbs**

1–2 teaspoons **yeast extract**

salt and **pepper**

Gravy:

300 ml (1 pint) **vegetable stock**

1½ teaspoons **soy sauce**

1 tablespoon **redcurrant jelly**

1½ teaspoons **cornflour**

1½ teaspoons **sherry**

PREP

30

COOK

50

SERVES

4

posh

mates

fab

savoury nut roast

If you want a change, why not add a tablespoon of curry powder at the end and serve with rice and mango chutney.

1 Heat the oven to 220°C (425°F), Gas Mark 7.

2 Grease a 20 cm (8 inch) square tin or shallow ovenproof dish.

3 Melt the butter or margarine in a large saucepan and fry the onions gently for 5–10 minutes, until soft. Add the nuts, breadcrumbs, herbs, yeast extract and a dash of salt and pepper.

4 Press the mixture into the tin or dish and smooth the top. Bake in the oven for 35–40 minutes.

5 Meanwhile, make the gravy. Boil up the stock, soy sauce and redcurrant jelly. Mix the cornflour with the sherry to make a paste. Stir a little of the hot gravy into the paste, then tip everything into the pan and simmer until thick.

6 Take the nut roast out of the tin and cut into wedges, then dish up with a good dollop of the veggie gravy.

mushroom toad-in-the-hole

This fantastically crunchy, more-ish dish is a real winner. The perfect brunch or lunch dish, and surprisingly simple to cook.

1 Heat the oven to 230°C (450°F), Gas Mark 8.

2 Put the mushrooms, stalk side up, in a large shallow ovenproof dish.

3 Melt the butter with 4 tablespoons of the oil in a frying pan. Add the garlic and herbs, a dash of salt and pepper and stir for about 30 seconds. Pour over the mushrooms and bake in the oven for 2 minutes.

4 Meanwhile, put the flour in a bowl and slowly whisk in the eggs, horseradish, milk and a dash of salt and pepper until really smooth.

5 Pour the batter over the mushrooms and bake for 20–25 minutes until the batter has risen and is golden.

6 At the same time, heat the rest of the oil in a frying pan. Add the onions and sugar and fry for 5 minutes until deep golden, then pour in the beer and stock and add a sprinkling of salt and pepper. Stir for 5 minutes.

7 Cut up the toad and pour the beer gravy generously over the top.

PREP

5

COOK

25

SERVES

4

yum!

telly

boozy

4 large **open mushrooms, or** 400 g (13 oz) smaller **open mushrooms**

25 g (1 oz) **butter**

5 tablespoons **olive oil**

3 **garlic cloves**, sliced

2 tablespoons **rosemary or thyme**, chopped

salt and **pepper**

125 g (4 oz) **plain flour**

2 **eggs**

2 tablespoons **horseradish sauce**

400 ml (14 fl oz) **milk**

Beer gravy:

2 **onions**, sliced

2 teaspoons **sugar**

275 ml (9 fl oz) **beer**

150 ml (¼ pint) **vegetable stock**

325 g (11 oz) **can borlotti beans**, drained and rinsed

400 g (13 oz) **can butter beans**, drained and rinsed

400 g (13 oz) **can flageolet beans**, drained and rinsed

400 g (13 oz) **passata**

1 large **onion**, chopped

2 teaspoons **dried mixed herbs**

2 teaspoons **parsley**, chopped

1 **garlic clove**, finely chopped

2 **red or green peppers**, cored, deseeded and chopped

pepper

a little **vegetable oil**, for greasing

2 **tomatoes**, chopped

3 tablespoons grated **Parmesan cheese**

PREP

10

COOK

35

SERVES

4

easy

yum!

share

easy bean and pepper bake

This dish is dead easy to make. Just bung it in the oven, put your feet up and in half-an-hour you'll have a tasty dinner ready.

1 Heat the oven to 180°C (350°F), Gas Mark 4.

2 Mix the beans, passata, onion, herbs, garlic, peppers and pepper in a bowl.

3 Grease an ovenproof dish with a little oil. Pour in the bean mix and spread the chopped tomatoes over the top.

4 Bake for 35–40 minutes, then sprinkle with Parmesan cheese, before dishing up with rice, broccoli and carrots.

chilli bean bake

PREP

15

COOK

50

SERVES

4

spicy

fab

mates

A spicy and nutritious bake – great to eat when vegging out in front of the telly.

3 tablespoons **vegetable oil**

1 **onion**, chopped

2 **garlic cloves**, crushed

150 g (5 oz) **mushrooms**, halved or quartered if large

2 teaspoons **mild chilli powder**

400 g (13 oz) **can red kidney beans**, drained and rinsed

250 ml (8 fl oz) **carrot juice**

2 tablespoons **tomato purée**

salt and **pepper**

750 g (1½ lb) **new potatoes**, sliced

50 g (2 oz) **Cheddar cheese**, grated

1 Heat the oven to 200°C (400°F), Gas Mark 6.

2 Heat the oil in a saucepan, add the onion and garlic and fry gently for 5 minutes. Add the mushrooms and fry for 2 more minutes.

3 Stir in the chilli powder, kidney beans, carrot juice, tomato purée and a little salt and pepper. Bring to the boil, then turn down the heat, cover and simmer gently for 5 minutes.

4 Meanwhile, boil the sliced potatoes for 5 minutes then drain.

5 Transfer the bean mix to a 1.8 litre (3 pint) or similar ovenproof dish. Layer the potatoes over the top and scatter the cheese on top of that. Bake for about 30 minutes until the top is golden, then eat with a mixed leaf salad or broccoli.

50 g (2 oz) **butter**

3 tablespoons **vegetable oil**

2 **aubergines**, thinly sliced

4 **potatoes**, thinly sliced

3 large **onions**, chopped

2 **garlic cloves**, chopped

3 large **tomatoes**, skinned and sliced

salt and **pepper**

Cheese sauce:

50 g (2 oz) **butter or margarine**

40 g (1½ oz) **plain flour**

600 ml (1 pint) **milk**

250g (8 oz) **Cheddar cheese**, grated

salt and **pepper**

1 teaspoon **mixed spice**

1 teaspoon **mustard**

PREP

15

COOK

120

SERVES

4

posh

cool

party

vegetable moussaka

A slight variation on the traditional Greek dish (see page 141). This is a really filling meal, so make sure you don't have to do anything but collapse on the sofa afterwards.

1 Heat the oven to 160°C (325°F), Gas Mark 3.

2 Heat half the butter with half the oil in a pan, add the aubergines and potatoes and cook for 10 minutes, turning. Put on a plate.

3 Heat the rest of the butter and oil, add the onions, garlic and tomatoes and cook gently for 10 minutes. Mix in half the aubergines and potatoes.

4 Make the sauce: heat the butter, add the flour and stir for 1–2 minutes. Slowly stir in the milk until you have a smooth sauce, then take it off the heat. Mix in most of the cheese, the mixed spice, mustard and salt and pepper.

5 Put half the mixed vegetables into an oven-proof dish, dollop half the sauce over then add the rest of the mixed vegetables. Put the rest of the aubergines and potatoes on top and then the rest of the sauce.

6 Cover the dish and bake in the oven for 1¼ hours. Take off the lid, chuck on the rest of the cheese, put the dish back in the oven and turn up the heat slightly. Bake for 10 more minutes, then serve right away.

vegetable curry

The coconut milk gives this a sumptuously creamy sauce, while the curry paste gives it oodles of attitude.

PREP

10

COOK

25

SERVES

4

cheap

fun

spicy

1 tablespoon **vegetable oil**

1 **onion**, chopped

1 **garlic clove**, crushed

2 tablespoons **curry paste**

1½ kg (3 lb) prepared **mixed vegetables** (such as courgettes, peppers, squash, mushrooms and green beans)

200 g (7 oz) **can chopped tomatoes**

400 g (13 oz) **can coconut milk**

2 tablespoons chopped **coriander leaves**

1 Heat the oil in a large saucepan, add the onion and garlic and fry for 2 minutes. Stir in the curry paste and fry for 1 more minute.

2 Add the mixed vegetables and fry for 2–3 minutes, stirring occasionally, then add the tomatoes and coconut milk. Stir well, bring to the boil, then lower the heat and simmer for 12–15 minutes until all the vegetables are cooked.

3 Stir in the coriander and dish up with a mound of rice and some naan bread.

450 g (14½ oz) **ready-rolled shortcrust pastry**, defrosted if frozen

vegetable oil, for greasing

Filling:

2 tablespoons **olive oil**

1 small **onion**, thinly sliced

2 **courgettes**, thinly sliced

250 g (8 oz) **cherry tomatoes**, halved

125 g (4 oz) **Cheddar cheese**, grated

2 tablespoons **milk**

2 **eggs**, beaten

½ teaspoon **dried mixed herbs**

salt and **pepper**

PREP

COOK

SERVES

share

fab

posh

courgette and cherry tomato flan

Great for when you fancy something really tasty yet healthy and it's bound to impress your mates.

1 Heat the oven to 200°C (400°F), Gas Mark 6.

2 Unfold the pastry and lay it over the inside of a greased 23 cm (9 inch) flan tin. Push gently into place and prick the base with a fork. Cover with a piece of greaseproof paper and fill the bottom with a layer of cheap dried beans, for example butter beans.

3 Bake in the oven for 10 minutes. Remove the paper and beans and bake for another 10–12 minutes until crisp and golden.

4 Meanwhile, heat the olive oil in a frying pan, add the onion and courgettes and fry gently for 5–6 minutes until lightly golden. Scatter the mixture over the base of the pastry case and top with the tomatoes.

5 Beat together the Cheddar, milk, eggs, herbs and salt and pepper and spread over the courgette mixture. Bake for 30–35 minutes until firm and golden.

veggie sausages and beans

These veggie sausages are great for breakfast, lunch or dinner, and you can always make more than you need and bung some in the freezer.

1 Soak the beans overnight in plenty of cold water. Drain, put in a pan and cover with fresh water. Bring to the boil and boil for 10 minutes, then turn down the heat and simmer for 30 minutes until tender. Drain and put in an ovenproof dish.

2 Heat the oven to 160°C (325°F), Gas Mark 3.

3 Mix the cornflour with 4 tablespoons of water until smooth. Add the stock and pour over the beans. Stir in the oil, tomatoes, onions, mustard and ketchup. Bake for 1½–2 hours until the beans are tender.

4 Make the sausage mix: cook the potatoes in boiling water for 5 minutes until soft. Drain then mash until creamy and smooth. Add the rest of the ingredients and mix well. Divide into 12 and shape into thick sausages.

5 Heat the oil in a frying pan and fry the sausages for about 10 minutes. Mound up the beans and stick the sausages on top.

*Plus overnight soaking

PREP

30*

COOK

120

SERVES

6

cool

beer

mates

250 g (8 oz) **dried haricot beans**

2 teaspoons **cornflour**

300 ml (½ pint) **vegetable stock**

2 tablespoons **olive oil**

400 g (13 oz) **can chopped tomatoes**

2 **onions**, chopped

1 teaspoon **mustard**

2 tablespoons **tomato ketchup**

Sausages:

300 g (10 oz) **potatoes**, cut into cubes

2 small **carrots**, grated

1 large **onion**, finely chopped

100 g (3½ oz) **Cheddar cheese**, grated

100 g (3½ oz) **breadcrumbs**

1 **egg**

salt and **pepper**

a little **oil** for frying

400 g (13 oz) **can flageolet, cannellini or red kidney beans**

375 g (12 oz) **sweet potato, carrot or parsnip**, cut into chunks

2 tablespoons **olive oil**

1 **onion**, chopped

2 **garlic cloves**, crushed

1 **celery stick**, finely chopped

1 tablespoon **plain flour**

1 tablespoon **tomato purée**

2 teaspoons **soy sauce**

To serve:

4 **baps, pitta breads or burger buns**

4 teaspoons **mayonnaise**

4 teaspoons **tomato ketchup**

handful of **lettuce leaves**

COOK

40

SERVES

4

juicy

snack

telly

veggie burgers

If you use sweet potato and/or red kidney beans these veggie burgers will have a lovely orange colour.

1 Drain the beans, rinse and dry on kitchen paper. Put in a bowl and mash well.

2 Boil the sweet potato, carrot or parsnip for 20–25 minutes until really tender, then drain and mash.

3 Heat 1 tablespoon of the oil in a large frying pan. Add the onion, garlic and celery, and fry for 5 minutes, stirring now and then. Add the mashed sweet potato, carrot or parsnip and cook, stirring, for another 5 minutes, then put in a large bowl and stir in the beans, flour, tomato purée and soy sauce.

4 Make 8 small or 4 large, thin burgers. Heat the rest of the oil in a frying pan and fry the burgers for 4 minutes, then turn and cook on the other side for another 3 minutes.

5 Meanwhile, split each bap, pitta bread or burger bun. Spread one side with mayonnaise, the other with tomato ketchup and chuck on some lettuce leaves, then put a burger in the middle and you have a meaty snack.

falafel

These savoury patties are a traditional Middle Eastern snack, and you can easily impress your mates with your exotic cuisine.

1 Drain the broad beans, dry them thoroughly, then mash them up really well in a bowl until they make a fairly smooth paste. Stir in all the other ingredients, except the oil, and add a dash of salt and pepper. Cover and chill for 1 hour.

2 Make the mix into 12 small patties. Heat a shallow layer of oil in a frying pan and fry the patties, a few at a time, for 1–2 minutes on each side until golden brown. These are delicious served hot with Greek yogurt flavoured with mint.

*Plus 1 hour chilling

PREP

COOK

MAKES

posh

mates

beer

125 g (4 oz) **frozen broad beans**, defrosted

2 tablespoons **Greek yogurt**

1 tablespoon **tahini paste**

1 tablespoon **lemon juice**

1 **garlic clove**, crushed

1 teaspoon **ground coriander**

½ teaspoon **cumin**

¼ teaspoon **cayenne pepper**

1 tablespoon chopped **coriander leaves**

1 tablespoon chopped **mint**

oil for frying

salt and **pepper**

ratatouille

125 ml (4 fl oz) **olive oil**

2 large **aubergines**, quartered lengthways and cut into chunks

2 **courgettes**, cut into chunks

2 large **red peppers**, cored, deseeded and cut into cubes

1 large **yellow pepper**, cored, deseeded and cut into cubes

2 large **onions**, thinly sliced

3 large **garlic cloves**, crushed

1 tablespoon **tomato purée**

400 g (13 oz) **can tomatoes**

12 **basil leaves**, torn

1 tablespoon **fresh mixed herbs**, finely chopped

1 tablespoon **paprika**

salt and **pepper**

2–4 tablespoons finely chopped **parsley**

COOK

30

SERVES
8

fast

easy

share

This is one of the great dishes of the Mediterranean, and by roasting the vegetables you get a really lush, rich sauce. You can have this with just about anything – hot or cold with crusty bread, as a pasta sauce or as a filling for omelettes.

1 Heat the oven to 220°C (425°F), Gas Mark 7.

2 Heat half the oil in a roasting tin and toss the aubergines, courgettes and peppers in the hot oil, then roast them in the oven for about 30 minutes, until tender.

3 Meanwhile, heat the rest of the oil in a large saucepan. Fry the onions and garlic over a medium heat, stirring occasionally, for 3–5 minutes, until soft but not coloured. Add the tomato purée, tomatoes, basil, mixed herbs and paprika and a sprinkling of salt and pepper. Stir well, then simmer for 10–15 minutes until thick and syrupy.

4 Drain the roasted vegetables on kitchen paper then add to the tomato mixture. Mix, then toss in the parsley, taste, and add a bit more salt and pepper if it needs it. Either eat straight away or you can have it cold.

cauliflower cheese

Cauliflower smothered in cheese – delicious! This makes a great winter lunch with lots of bread and maybe some soup, or serve it with nut loaf for a really filling meal. Just make sure you don't need to do anything too energetic afterwards.

1 Boil the cauliflower for about 12 minutes until tender. Drain and put in an oven-proof dish.

2 Melt the butter in a saucepan, stir in the flour and cook for 1 minute. Slowly stir in the milk, then the cheese and heat, stirring all the time until thick. Sprinkle with salt and pepper.

3 Pour the sauce over the cauliflower and scatter the breadcrumbs over the top. Put under a medium grill until the top is golden brown, and dish up with bread.

PREP

10

COOK

15

SERVES

2

cheap

yum!

snack

1 small **cauliflower**, divided into florets

15 g (½ oz) **butter**

2 tablespoons **plain flour**

150 ml (¼ pint) **milk**

40 g (1½ oz) **Cheddar cheese**, grated

salt and **pepper**

1 tablespoon **breadcrumbs**

250 g (8 oz) **small tomatoes**, red and yellow plum ones if possible

250 g (8 oz) **thin green beans**, trimmed

handful of **mint**, chopped

1 **garlic clove**, crushed

4 tablespoons **olive oil**

1 tablespoon **balsamic vinegar**

salt and **pepper**

PREP

COOK

SERVES

fresh

fast

snack

tomato and green bean salad

This simple, sexy salad transforms humble vegetables into something truly delicious.

1 Cut the tomatoes in half and put in a bowl.

2 Boil the green beans for 2 minutes, then drain and add to the tomatoes.

3 Chuck in the mint, garlic, olive oil and balsamic vinegar, add a dash of salt and pepper and mix everything together. Eat warm or leave until cold. Sublime!

mushroom bruschetta

These tasty toasties are quick to put together, then all you need is a mixed leaf salad and a cold glass of wine and you have the perfect dinner (or boozy lunch!).

1 Cut the ciabatta into 3 or 4 slices. Toast both sides until just brown, then spread on the tomato or olive paste.

2 Mix together the tomato, mushrooms, olive oil and pesto and sprinkle over some salt and pepper. Spoon the mixture over the toast and scatter the Parmesan over the top.

3 Put the bruschetta under a hot grill until they are really hot.

PREP

10

COOK

5

SERVES

1

easy

fab

party

1 **ciabatta roll**

2 teaspoons **sun-dried tomato or black olive paste**

1 **tomato**, chopped

4 **small mushrooms**, chopped

1 tablespoon **olive oil**

1 teaspoon **pesto**

salt and **pepper**

2 tablespoons grated **Parmesan cheese**

meals for mates

chicken fajitas

PREP

15*

COOK

45

SERVES

4

easy

cool

share

2 boneless, skinless **chicken breasts**, cut into wide strips

2 tablespoons **olive oil**

2 large **onions**, sliced

1 **red pepper**, cored, deseeded and cut into strips

1 **green pepper**, cored, deseeded and cut into strips

12 **wheat tortillas**, warmed

250 g (8 oz) **guacamole**

300 ml (½ pint) **soured cream**

1 tablespoon **coriander leaves**, chopped

Marinade:

juice of 4 **limes**

3 tablespoons **olive oil**

1 teaspoon dried **oregano**

1 tablespoon **coriander leaves**

These are great party food as everyone can make their own – just cook everything up and have big bowls filled with salsa, chilli, guacamole and sour cream that people can dollop onto their Mexican pancakes as they wish.

1 Make the marinade: mix the lime juice with the olive oil, oregano and coriander in a bowl. Add the chicken strips and stir well. Cover and put in the fridge for 4 hours.

2 Heat the oven to 200°C (400°C), Gas Mark 6.

3 Put the chicken strips and marinade into a roasting pan. Cover with foil and bake in the oven for 30 minutes, then take off the foil and bake for another 15 minutes. When cooked, slice into very thin strips.

4 Meanwhile, heat the olive oil and fry the onions and peppers until soft.

5 Chuck some of the onions and peppers onto each warm tortilla then top with chicken. Add a big dollop of guacamole and sour cream, sprinkle with coriander and roll up like a pancake. Lovely!

*Plus 4 hours marinating

marinated chicken kebabs

PREP

15*

COOK

15

SERVES

4

mates

party

fab

If you think that kebabs are only suitable for eating after a big, boozy night out, then these delicious chicken kebabs will make you think again.

1 Make the marinade: mix the lime juice, honey, chilli and olive oil in a bowl until smooth.

2 Cut the chicken into long strips. Add the chicken to the marinade and stir until it is covered. Cover and put in the fridge for at least 1 hour and longer if you want.

3 Spear the chicken onto skewers and cover with the marinade, then cook under a hot grill, turning occasionally, until the chicken is cooked, tender and golden brown. Brush the kebabs with more marinade if they look like they are getting too dry or are burning.

4 Meanwhile, make the avocado sauce: mix the olive oil and vinegar in a bowl, beat in the avocado until the mixture is thick and smooth. Stir in the tomato and spring onions, then the soured cream. Dish up the kebabs with a dollop of avocado sauce.

*Plus at least 1 hour marinating

6 boneless, skinless **chicken breasts**

Marinade:

juice of 2 **limes**

1 tablespoon **honey**

1 **green chilli**, deseeded and finely chopped

2 tablespoons **olive oil**

Avocado sauce:

3 tablespoons **olive oil**

1 tablespoon **red wine vinegar**

1 large **avocado**, peeled, stoned and mashed

1 large **tomato**, skinned, deseeded and chopped

2 **spring onions**, chopped

125 ml (4 fl oz) **soured cream**

4 **chicken quarters**

2 **lemons**, cut in half

1 tablespoon **dried oregano**

2 **thyme sprigs**

4 tablespoons **olive oil**

4 **garlic cloves**, roughly chopped

Yogurt sauce:

250 ml (8 fl oz) **Greek yogurt**

1–2 **garlic cloves**

½ teaspoon **salt**

1 tablespoon **dill**, chopped

PREP

COOK

SERVES

fresh

posh

fun

lemon chicken with yogurt sauce

This really will remind you of holidays in the Mediterranean. This chicken is always tender, moist and very tasty, and all you need to accompany it is a Greek salad, or chips for an unhealthy but pleasurable meal.

1 Rub the chicken quarters all over, quite hard, with the cut lemons. Place in a large ovenproof dish, add the oregano, thyme, olive oil, garlic and rubbed lemon halves and mix everything together well. Cover and marinate for at least 2 hours.

2 Meanwhile, make the yogurt sauce. Pour the yogurt into a bowl and beat. Mash together the garlic and salt and stir into the yoghurt with the dill.

3 Take the chicken out of the dish and bake the pieces under a medium-hot grill for about 30 minutes, spooning a bit of the marinade over the chicken now and then if it looks too dry or burnt.

4 Check the chicken is cooked through by piercing the thickest bit with a knife – if the juices are clear it is ready. Dish up with the yogurt sauce and a big plate of chips.

*Plus at least 2 hours marinating

tequila chicken in a pine nut sauce

Although this may sound like rather a weird recipe to you, the gingernut biscuits in this Mexican dish add a great flavour as well as thickening the sauce.

PREP

30

COOK

45

SERVES

4

party

mates

boozy

4 tablespoons **vegetable oil**

4 pieces of **chicken**, preferably leg joints, skinned

2 **garlic cloves**, chopped

4 **tomatoes**, skinned and chopped

300 ml (½ pint) **chicken stock**

few drops **Tabasco sauce or** a pinch of **chilli powder**

2 **gingernut biscuits**

50 g (2 oz) **raisins**

2 tablespoons **tequila or sherry**

3 tablespoons **pine nuts**

salt and **pepper**

1 Heat 2 tablespoons of oil in a frying pan then fry the chicken for 10 minutes, turning once or twice. Remove from the pan and put on a plate.

2 Heat the rest of the oil and fry the garlic and tomatoes for a few minutes.

3 Meanwhile, mix the chicken stock with the Tabasco or chilli powder and pour over the gingernut biscuits. When the biscuits are slightly softened, mash them into the stock and stir until smooth.

4 Pour the biscuit mix into the pan with the garlic and tomatoes, stir well, then add the chicken and raisins.

5 Cover the pan and simmer for about 10 minutes or until the chicken is tender. Add a glug of tequila or sherry, chuck in the pine nuts and some salt and pepper if it needs it. Heat for a further 2 minutes, then dish up with tortilla chips.

1 hot **red chilli**, deseeded and finely chopped

2 **garlic cloves**, crushed

2.5 cm (1 inch) piece of **fresh root ginger**, peeled and finely chopped

2 tablespoons **lemon juice**

1 tablespoon **coriander seeds**

1 tablespoon **cumin seeds**

2 teaspoons **garam masala**

6 tablespoons **natural yogurt**

a few drops each of **red** and **yellow food colouring**

salt

4 pieces of skinless **chicken on the bone**

To top:

lemon wedges

coriander sprigs

PREP
20*

COOK
30

SERVES
4

spicy

yum!

beer

tandoori chicken

You can easily leave out the food colouring as it doesn't affect the taste, but if you want the scarily artificial but authentic Indian take-away look then you need to add it!

1 Mix the chilli, garlic, ginger, lemon juice and spices to make a paste.

2 Put the paste in a large, shallow ovenproof dish. Add the yogurt, food colouring and a dash of salt and mix well.

3 Cut the flesh of the chicken deeply (right down to the bone) with a sharp knife. Put the chicken in a single layer in the dish, then spoon the marinade over the chicken and push it into the cuts in the flesh. Cover and marinate in the fridge for at least 4 hours, but overnight is best.

4 Cook the chicken under a medium-hot grill, turning often, for about 30 minutes or until the juices run clear when pierced with a knife. Dish up with rice or salad and garnish with a few lemon wedges and coriander sprigs dotted on top.

*Plus at least 4 hours marinating

peppered chicken skewers

A heavenly dish. If you want a quick fix then this healthy snack is ideal. Best cooked on the barbecue, this also tastes great when grilled, and why not make some veggie kebabs to go with it?

1 Put a chicken breast in a clean plastic bag or between 2 sheets of cling film, then flatten it a bit with a rolling pin or wine bottle. Do the same with the rest of the chicken breasts then cut into thick strips.

2 Put the chicken strips in a bowl and add the rest of the ingredients. Mix well, then cover and marinate for 5–10 minutes.

3 Spear the chicken strips onto about eight skewers and cook under a medium-hot grill for 4–5 minutes on each side or until the chicken is cooked through. Eat at once with a mixed leaf salad.

*Plus 5–10 minutes marinating

PREP

10*

COOK

10

SERVES

4

fast

juicy

posh

4 boneless, skinless **chicken breasts**

2 tablespoons **rosemary**, finely chopped

2 **garlic cloves**, finely chopped

3 tablespoons **lemon juice**

2 teaspoons **mustard**

1 tablespoon **honey**

2 teaspoons freshly ground **black pepper**

1 tablespoon **olive oil**

a pinch of **salt**

2 tablespoons **olive oil**

250 g (8 oz) boneless, skinless **chicken breasts**, diced

1 large **onion**, finely chopped

3 **celery sticks**, diced

2 **carrots** diced

2 teaspoons **dried oregano**

125 ml (4 fl oz) **red wine**

400 g (13 oz) **can chopped tomatoes**

salt and **pepper**

375 g (12 oz) **penne pasta**

PREP

10

COOK

20

SERVES

4

easy

mates

saucy

chicken and tomato pasta

This is a great dish if you want to knock up a tasty meal for you and your mates. It's dead easy to make and it only requires a few fresh ingredients – the rest you'll probably already have in your cupboard.

1 Heat the oil in a frying pan and fry the chicken pieces, stirring occasionally, until lightly coloured. Add the onion, celery and carrots and cook for 5 minutes until softened.

2 Add the oregano, wine and tomatoes and season with a bit of salt and pepper. Bring the sauce to the boil, cover the pan and simmer for 10 minutes.

3 Meanwhile, cook the pasta according to packet instructions. Drain it and put it back in the saucepan, then mix in the sauce. Dish it up and tuck in.

chicken and broccoli risotto

Make sure you keep an eye on this risotto all the time so that it cooks evenly and doesn't stick to the pan. If you do this then you should have the most soothing of dishes – soft rice with a bit of firmness, and a moist, creamy sauce. Luscious!

1 Melt a third of the butter with the oil in a saucepan, add the chicken and fry over a low heat for 2–3 minutes. Add the onion and fry for 5 minutes until it is soft but not coloured. Add the garlic and chilli and fry until the garlic is golden.

2 Add the rice to the pan and stir for 1–2 minutes. Add the hot stock, a glug at a time, stirring constantly and letting the liquid be absorbed before adding more. This will take about 25 minutes, which will leave the rice creamy but firm.

3 Drop the broccoli florets into a saucepan of boiling water and boil for 1 minute. Drain and add to the rice with the Parmesan. Add a dash of salt and pepper, stir in the rest of the butter and eat immediately with a glass of cold dry white wine.

PREP

10

COOK

35

SERVES

6

share

posh

fresh

40 g (1½ oz) **butter**

2 tablespoons **olive oil**

2 boneless, skinless **chicken breasts**, cut into cubes

½ **onion**, very finely chopped

1 **garlic clove**, finely chopped

1–2 **fresh red chillies**, deseeded and very finely chopped

500 g (1 lb) **risotto rice**

1 litre (1¾ pints) boiling **chicken stock**

250 g (8 oz) **broccoli** florets

3 tablespoons **Parmesan cheese**, grated

salt and **pepper**

2 teaspoons **vegetable oil**

1 large **onion**, chopped

250 g (8 oz) **can pinto beans**, drained and rinsed

300 g (10 oz) cooked **chicken breast**, skinned and cut into cubes

4 green chillies, deseeded and chopped

1 teaspoon **dried oregano**

1 large **tomato**, chopped

¼ teaspoon **chilli powder**

¼ teaspoon ground **cumin**

400 g (13 oz) **passata**

12 **wheat tortillas**

250 g (8 oz) **ready-made salsa**

75 g (3 oz) **mozzarella cheese**, grated

PREP

COOK

SERVES

party

spicy

boozy

chicken enchiladas with salsa

The perfect food to accompany a tequila party. Carry on the Mexican theme with some guacamole (see page 77) and a few strong cocktails or tequila shots. Mango salsa tastes especially good with this recipe.

1 Heat the oven to 180°C (350°F), Gas Mark 4.

2 Heat the oil in a saucepan, add the onion and fry for about 5 minutes until soft. Stir in the beans, chicken, chillies, oregano and fresh tomato and heat through. Then put on one side.

3 Put the chilli powder, cumin and passata in a saucepan and simmer for 2 minutes, then take off the heat.

4 Dip each tortilla into the tomato mix and put on a plate. Fill each one with 3 tablespoons of the chicken mix. Roll up and put in an ovenproof dish. Pour two thirds of the salsa over the top and sprinkle with cheese.

5 Bake in the oven for about 20 minutes, then dish up with rest of the salsa.

one pan chicken

This is so simple to make – just bung everything in together, pop it in the oven, relax with a beer, and an hour later you have a really tasty meal.

1 Heat the oven to 200°C (400°F), Gas Mark 6.

2 Make two or three cuts into each piece of chicken, then put the chicken pieces in a roasting tin.

3 Chuck the vegetables into the roasting tin. Glug over the olive oil and add the garlic. Sprinkle with the sage, salt, pepper and Cajun spice.

4 Roast in the oven for 45 minutes. Turn the chicken over, spoon the oil over the potatoes and drizzle with the honey. Cook for 15 more minutes until the chicken is thoroughly cooked, then eat while still hot.

PREP

20

COOK

60

SERVES
4

easy

yum!

juicy

4 **chicken thighs** and 4 **chicken drumsticks**

1 kg (2 lb) baby **new potatoes**

1 small **butternut squash**, peeled, deseeded and cut into slices

1 **red pepper**, deseeded and cut into chunks

4 tablespoons **olive oil**

1 whole **garlic bulb**, separated into cloves but unpeeled

1–2 tablespoons **fresh sage leaves or a little dried sage**

salt and **pepper**

1 teaspoon **ground Cajun spice**

4 teaspoons **honey**

500 g (1 lb) **spaghetti**

pepper

50 g (2 oz) **Parmesan cheese**, grated

Meat sauce:

4 tablespoons **vegetable oil**

1 **onion**, finely chopped

1 **garlic clove**, crushed

4 **rashers rindless bacon**, chopped

1 **carrot**, cut into cubes

1 **celery stick**, cut into cubes

500 g (1 lb) **beef mince**

150 ml (¼ pint) **red wine**

salt and **pepper**

125 ml (4 fl oz) **milk**

400 g (13 oz) **can chopped tomatoes**

1 tablespoon **sugar**

1 teaspoon **chopped oregano**

PREP

15

COOK

90

spaghetti bolognese

The beautiful city of Bologna, which gives this recipe its name, is renowned for its fine pasta. Serve with garlic pizza bread and salad for a truly authentic Italian meal.

SERVES

4

fun

1 Make the meat sauce: heat the oil in a saucepan and fry the onion, garlic, bacon, carrot and celery until soft and golden. Add the mince and cook, stirring occasionally, until brown. Add the red wine and bring to the boil. Turn the heat down and cook over a medium heat until most of the wine has evaporated, then add a dash of salt and pepper.

2 Add the milk and stir well until the milk has been absorbed.

cheap

3 Add the tomatoes, sugar and oregano, turn down the heat and simmer, uncovered, for at least 1 hour, stirring occasionally, until the sauce has reduced.

4 Cook the spaghetti according to the packet instructions. Drain well and sprinkle with pepper. Mound up the spaghetti, add a good dollop of Bolognese, then sprinkle with Parmesan and enjoy.

easy

lasagne

If you want to try something different to the usual beef lasagne, make a chicken one instead. It's really simple – just use chicken mince instead of beef mince, and a mixture of half-milk/half-yogurt in the cheese sauce.

1 First make the meat sauce. Heat the oil in a large saucepan and fry the onions for 3–5 minutes, until soft. Add the garlic and fry for 1 more minute, then stir in the herbs, tomato purée and beef. Fry, stirring constantly, for 5 minutes. Add the tomatoes and a dash of salt and pepper. Stir well, then cover the pan and simmer for 45 minutes, stirring occasionally.

2 Meanwhile, make the cheese sauce. Melt the butter in a saucepan. Stir in the flour and cook for 1 minute. Add the milk slowly, whisking over a medium heat until thick. Add the Cheddar cheese, stir well until it has melted, then stir in a pinch of salt and pepper.

3 Heat the oven to 190°C (375°F), Gas Mark 5.

4 Grease a 1.8 litre (3 pint) ovenproof dish. Spoon one-third of the meat mixture over the base. Spread over a quarter of the cheese sauce and cover with 3 sheets of lasagne. Do the same twice more, finishing with a layer of pasta. Cover with the rest of the cheese sauce and sprinkle Parmesan over the top. Bake in the oven for 1 hour. Dish up with a green salad and crusty bread to mop up the juices.

PREP

60

COOK

60

SERVES

4

mates

fab

share

9 sheets ready-to-cook **lasagne**

50 g (2 oz) **Parmesan cheese**, grated

Meat sauce:

2 tablespoons **vegetable oil**

2 **onions**, chopped finely

3 **garlic cloves**, crushed

1 tablespoon **dried oregano**

1 tablespoon **dried basil**

3 tablespoons **tomato purée**

500 g (1 lb) **beef mince**

400 g (13 oz) **can tomatoes**

salt and **pepper**

Cheese sauce:

25 g (1 oz) **butter**

25 g (1 oz) **plain flour**

600 ml (1 pint) **milk**

250 g (8 oz) **Cheddar cheese**, grated

salt and **pepper**

1–2 tablespoons **olive oil**

500 g (1 lb) **chicken mince**

1 **onion**, sliced

1 **carrot**, sliced

150 ml (¼ pint) **white wine**

300 ml (½ pint) **chicken stock**

salt and **pepper**

125 g (4 oz) **spinach**, cooked and chopped

2–3 tablespoons **single cream**

12 ready-to-cook **cannelloni tubes**

425 g (14 oz) **passata**

40 g (1½ oz) **Parmesan cheese**, grated

PREP

COOK

SERVES

share

posh

yum!

chicken cannelloni

One for the girls. Invite round a few friends, pop this in the oven while you pamper yourselves, then crack open a bottle of wine and get a soppy video to watch.

1 Heat the oil in a saucepan and fry the mince until golden brown then put in a bowl. Add the vegetables to the pan and cook until lightly coloured, then tip the mince back into the pan. Add the wine and stock and a dash of salt and pepper, then simmer gently for 40–45 minutes.

2 Heat the oven to 180°C (350°C), Gas Mark 4.

3 Stir the chopped spinach into the chicken with enough cream to soften the mixture.

4 Spoon the filling into the cannelloni tubes. Put in a greased ovenproof dish and pour the passata over the top. Bake in the oven for about 40 minutes.

5 Sprinkle a little Parmesan over the top and bake for another 5–10 minutes, then dish up with a mixed salad.

beef stroganoff

The perfect meal for a retro 70s night – just make sure you have your Abba CD ready.

1 Heat the oil in a frying pan and fry the onions until brown, stirring all the time. Gradually add the meat and stir until completely brown – if the pan isn't big enough do it in two batches.

2 When all the meat is brown, sprinkle with salt and pepper then add the gherkins, capers, beetroot, mushrooms and sugar.

3 Stir well, add stock and cover the pan. Simmer for 30 minutes or longer, then stir in the soured cream right at the end.

4 Mound up some rice and dollop the stroganoff on top.

fab

saucy

keeps

3 tablespoons **vegetable oil**

2 **onions**, sliced

875 g (1¾ lb) **stewing beef**, cut into strips

salt and **pepper**

125 g (4 oz) **gherkins**, sliced

2 tablespoons **capers**

4 tablespoons **bottled beetroot**, sliced

50 g (2 oz) **button mushrooms**

1 teaspoon **sugar**

150 ml (¼ pint) **beef stock**

4 tablespoons **soured cream**

1 tablespoon **vegetable oil**

4 **rashers rindless bacon**, chopped

1 **onion**, chopped

500 g (1 lb) **lamb mince**

1 teaspoon **dried oregano**

2 tablespoons **parsley**, chopped

150 ml (¼ pint) **red wine**

425 g (14 oz) **passata**

salt and **pepper**

750 g (1½ lb) **potatoes**, cooked and thinly sliced

25 g (1 oz) **butter**, melted

PREP

15

COOK

75

SERVES

4

posh

cheap

easy

fancy shepherd's pie

Instead of having the usual creamy mashed potato dolloped over the mince, this dish has layers of potatoes 'scalloped' on top.

1 Heat the oil in a frying pan, add the bacon and onion and fry for about 5 minutes, until soft. Add the lamb and fry, stirring, until brown all over.

2 Stir in the herbs, wine, passata and a dash of salt and pepper. Bring to the boil, then turn down the heat and simmer, uncovered, for about 25 minutes, until the lamb is tender and the sauce thick.

3 Heat the oven to 200°C (400°F), Gas Mark 6.

4 Put the meat into a greased 1.2 litre (2 pint) or similar ovenproof dish. Layer the potato slices over the top, overlapping for a scalloped effect, and drizzle with melted butter. Bake in the oven for 25 minutes, until the potato is golden brown. Dish up with vegetables such as broccoli, peas or carrots.

moussaka

This Greek dish is mouthwateringly good! Feed this to your mates and they'll definitely be impressed.

PREP

20

COOK

100

SERVES

4

juicy

mates

fab

3 tablespoons **vegetable oil**

3 large **onions**, thinly sliced

2 **aubergines**, thinly sliced

500 g (1 lb) **beef or lamb mince**

1 tablespoon **plain flour**

1 tablespoon **tomato purée**

300 ml (½ pint) **beef stock**

1 teaspoon **dried mixed herbs**

salt and **pepper**

6 **tomatoes**, sliced

Cheese sauce:

40 g (1½ oz) **butter or margarine**

40 g (1½ oz) **plain flour**

600 ml (1 pint) **milk**

75 g (3 oz) **Cheddar cheese**, grated

1 Heat the oil in a frying pan and fry the onion until soft. Remove from the pan and put on a plate.

2 Fry the aubergine slices in the pan, a few slices at a time, until golden on each side. Drain on kitchen paper.

3 Fry the meat until brown. Stir in the flour, tomato purée, stock, herbs and a dash of salt. Bring the mixture to the boil, then simmer for 15 minutes.

4 Meanwhile, make the cheese sauce. Melt the butter in a saucepan. Stir in the flour and cook for 1 minute. Add the milk slowly, whisking over a medium heat until thick. Add the Cheddar cheese, stir well until melted, then stir in a pinch of salt and pepper.

5 Heat the oven to 180°C (350°C), Gas Mark 4.

6 Layer the meat and the onions, aubergines and tomatoes in an ovenproof dish, then top with the cheese sauce. Bake in the oven for 1 hour then dish up with crusty bread or chips.

2 slices **bread**, crusts removed

75 ml (3 fl oz) **milk**

4 tablespoons **vegetable oil**

1 small **onion**, chopped, or 6 **spring onions**

1 **garlic clove**, chopped

750 g (1½ lb) **beef mince**

2 tablespoons **Parmesan cheese**, grated

salt and **pepper**

300 ml (½ pint) **white wine**

400 g (13 oz) **can chopped tomatoes**

PREP

20

COOK

80

SERVES

4

cool

mates

juicy

italian meatballs

This is a great way to jazz up mince and cook something similar but different to the perennial spaghetti Bolognese. Simply serve on a bed of rice or pasta for a delicious supper.

1 Heat the oven to 180°C (350°F), Gas Mark 4.

2 Put the bread in a bowl, pour in the milk and leave to soak.

3 Heat half the oil in a frying pan and fry the onions and garlic for 5 minutes until soft and just starting to go brown.

4 Mix the meat and milky bread together, then mix in the onion, garlic, Parmesan, salt and pepper until smooth. With clean wet hands, roll the mixture into 28 balls.

5 Heat the rest of the oil in a large frying pan and fry the meatballs in batches until brown, then put in a shallow ovenproof dish.

6 Pour the wine and tomatoes into the frying pan and bring to the boil, scraping the cooking juices up from the bottom of the pan. Sprinkle with salt and pepper and boil rapidly for 5 minutes.

7 Dollop the sauce over the meatballs, cover with foil and bake in the oven for about 1 hour until tender. Pile the meatballs and sauce on top of rice, pasta or noodles. Lovely!

spicy meat and bean pasta

PREP

20

COOK

60

SERVES

2

This delicious dish is so straightforward to make that you really should try it. It makes a great rustic dinner especially served with a bottle of hearty red wine.

1 Heat the oil in a saucepan, add the onion, carrot, garlic and lamb and fry for 5 minutes, stirring until the mince is brown all over.

2 Add the spices, tomatoes, stock, and a dash of salt and pepper. Bring to the boil, mixing everything together well.

3 Cover and simmer for 1 hour, stirring from time to time so it doesn't stick. Add extra stock if it gets too dry.

4 Cook the pasta according to the instructions on the packet.

5 Meanwhile, boil the green and broad beans for 5–7 minutes until just tender, then drain and sprinkle with the fresh herbs.

6 Drain the pasta, stir in the mince, mix well, then dish up and dollop the herby beans over the top. Enjoy.

share

spicy

snack

1 tablespoon **vegetable oil**

1 **onion**, finely chopped

2 **carrots**, about 250 g (8 oz) chopped

2 **garlic cloves**, crushed

250 g (8 oz) **lamb mince**

1 teaspoon **ground cinnamon**

½ teaspoon **ground allspice or nutmeg**

400 g (13 oz) **can chopped tomatoes**

300 ml (½ pint) **lamb stock**

salt and **pepper**

250 g (8 oz) **pasta**

100 g (3½ oz) **green beans**, halved

100 g (3½ oz) **frozen broad beans**

small bunch mixed **fresh mint** and **parsley**, chopped

beer-braised beef with cheese dumplings

boozy

juicy

share

Real pub food. A sumptuous rich sauce and filling dumplings make the perfect Sunday lunch – all you need is a pint of beer and time to sleep off the effects afterwards.

2 tablespoons **vegetable oil**

2 **onions**, sliced

750 g (1½ lb) **stewing beef**, cut into cubes

1 tablespoon **plain flour**

1 teaspoon **brown sugar**

300 ml (½ pint) **brown ale**

salt and **pepper**

Dumplings:

125 g (4 oz) **self-raising flour**

50 g (2 oz) melted **margarine**

25 g (1 oz) **Cheddar cheese**, grated

2–3 tablespoons **water**

1 Heat the oven to 180°C (350°F), Gas Mark 4.

2 Heat the oil in a saucepan and fry the onions until soft, then put them in an oven-proof dish.

3 Fry the beef in the saucepan until brown all over. Tip in the flour and let it all cook for 1 minute, stirring. Add the sugar, then gradually glug in the ale. Stir well, add a dash of salt and pepper, then add to the onion mix.

4 Cover the dish and cook in the oven for 30 minutes, then turn down the temperature to 160°C (325°F), Gas Mark 3 and cook for another 40 minutes.

5 Meanwhile, make the dumplings. Mix together the flour, margarine and cheese in a bowl. Add the water slowly, adding a bit more if needed to make a loose dough. Put a little flour on your hands, break the dough into 8 small bits, then roll into little balls.

6 Check the meat. If the casserole seems dry, add a little water or ale. Put the dumplings on top of the meat and cook for 20–30 minutes without a lid, until they have risen.

lamb casserole with red wine and herbs

A great Sunday lunch – it cooks so slowly there's time to pop out and have a few drinks with your mates, then come back to the most delicious and filling of meals.

1 Put the lamb in a large ovenproof dish with the onion, garlic, tomatoes, mixed herbs, orange rind, and a dash of salt and pepper. Glug the wine over the top, add the oil and stir well. Cover and leave to marinate in the fridge for 4 hours.

2 Heat the oven to 200°C (400°F), Gas Mark 6.

3 Fry the bacon for a couple of minutes until slightly brown, then put in the casserole with the chicken stock and mix well. Add a pinch of salt. Cover with a close-fitting lid or foil, making sure the liquid can't evaporate.

4 Cook in the oven for 1 hour, then turn down the heat to 180°C (350°F), Gas Mark 4 and cook for another 2 hours, adding a little water if it looks like it is drying out.

5 Dish up on top of rice, noodles or garlicky mashed potato, and sprinkle the olives and parsley over the top.

*Plus 4 hours marinating

PREP

15*

COOK

180

SERVES
4

mates

keeps

posh

1.25 kg (2½ lb) **shoulder of lamb**, boned, fat removed and cut into cubes

1 large **onion**, finely chopped

2 **garlic cloves**, crushed

2 large **tomatoes**, chopped

1 teaspoon **dried mixed herbs**

rind of 1 **orange**, cut into thin strips

salt and **pepper**

1 bottle of **red wine**

2 tablespoons **olive oil**

250 g (8 oz) **rindless bacon**, cut into cubes

300 ml (½ pint) **chicken stock**

75 g (3 oz) **black olives**

1 tablespoon chopped **parsley**

burritos with pork stuffing

1 kg (2 lb) boneless rolled **pork shoulder**

1 tablespoon **vegetable oil**

salt

350 ml (12 fl oz) **meat stock**

250 ml (8 fl oz) **tomato purée**

½ teaspoon grated **orange rind**

1 teaspoon **dried chilli flakes**

8 **wheat tortillas**

To top:

soured cream

½ **avocado**, stoned, peeled and finely sliced

1 teaspoon **dried chilli flakes**

Great snack food for a party. This fiery Mexican dish will inflame the taste buds and delight your friends.

1 Heat the oven to 180°C (350°F), Gas Mark 4.

2 Put the pork in a roasting tin and brush with a little oil. Sprinkle with salt, and roast for about 1½ hours, or until crisp and golden.

3 Meanwhile, make the sauce. Pour the stock into a saucepan with the tomato purée, orange rind and dried chilli flakes. Bring to the boil, turn down the heat and simmer for about 30 minutes until the sauce is thick.

4 Cut any fat off the cooked pork and tear the meat into shreds. Chuck the pork into the sauce and heat very gently over a low heat.

5 Pop the tortillas in the oven for a couple of minutes to warm. Put a little of the pork mixture into the centre of each tortilla and roll them up.

6 Dollop soured cream on top of the burritos, then pile on the avocado, and sprinkle chilli flakes over the top.

sweet-and-sour pork

This can easily be made with chicken or prawns instead of pork, or for a vegetarian option just add a few other vegetables such as carrots, bean sprouts and mangetout.

1 Heat the oil in a wok or large frying pan until really hot. Add the pork and onion and stir-fry over a high heat for about 2 minutes.

2 Add the tomato, cucumber, pineapple and pepper and stir-fry for another 3 minutes.

3 Add the sweet-and-sour sauce, mix well, stirring constantly for 1 minute, then dish up with rice or noodles.

PREP

10

COOK

10

SERVES

2

fresh

fruity

yum!

4 tablespoons **vegetable oil**

250 g (8 oz) **pork**, cut into thin slices

1½ **onions**, sliced

2 **tomatoes**, quartered

½ **cucumber**, cut into chunks

125 g (4 oz) **pineapple chunks**

1 **green or red pepper**, cored, deseeded and thinly sliced

200 ml (7 fl oz) **ready-made sweet-and-sour sauce**

500 g (1 lb) **sausages**

2 tablespoons **olive oil**

1 **onion**, finely chopped

2 **garlic cloves**, finely chopped

425 g (14 oz) **passata**

150 ml (¼ pint) **red wine**

6 **sun-dried tomatoes**, chopped

1 tablespoon chopped **rosemary**

2 tablespoons chopped **sage**

salt and **pepper**

sausage ragout

This makes such a tasty supper that you'll be hoping there's enough left for you to snack on the next morning.

1 Squeeze the sausages out of their skins into a bowl and break up with a fork.

2 Heat the oil in a saucepan and fry the onion and garlic for 5 minutes until soft and golden. Stir in the sausagemeat and cook until brown all over, keep breaking up any lumps that form.

3 Pour in the passata and wine and add the rest of the ingredients. Stir well and bring to the boil. Turn down the heat, cover the pan and simmer on a low heat for at least 1 hour until the sauce has reduced by about half. Add a good dash of salt and pepper, mix, then dish up the ragout with grilled polenta, pasta or gnocchi.

fun

juicy

yum!

paella

Paella is just so colourful, fragrant and full of flavour that it isn't surprising that it is Spain's most popular dish! If you can't be bothered with the fiddly preparation that mussels and prawns need then you can buy ready-prepared seafood at the supermarket.

1 Heat the oil in a frying pan and fry the chicken and bacon until golden and tender. Take out of the pan and put on a plate.

2 Fry the onion and garlic for 5 minutes until golden brown. Add the tomatoes and cook for 2–3 minutes, then add the red pepper and rice. Stir over a low heat for 1–2 minutes, mixing well.

3 Drop the saffron into the boiling water to infuse, then pour over the rice, then add a dash of salt and pepper.

4 Simmer until the rice is almost tender. Stir and make sure that there is enough water so that it doesn't dry out. Add more boiling water if it needs it.

5 Add the chicken mix to the pan and continue cooking until almost ready.

spicy

6 Add the sausage, mussels and prawns. Taste, and add more salt and pepper if it needs it. Heat for about 6 minutes then dish up straight from the paella pan.

share

fab

2 tablespoons **vegetable oil**

250 g (8 oz) **boneless chicken thighs**, cut into pieces

125 g (4 oz) **rindless bacon**, cut into cubes

1 large **onion**, chopped

2–3 **garlic cloves**

500 g (1 lb) **tomatoes**, skinned and chopped

1 **red pepper**, cored, deseeded and sliced

250–300 g (8–10 oz) **risotto rice**

¼ teaspoon **saffron powder or strands**

600 ml (1 pint) boiling **water**

salt and **pepper**

75 g (3 oz) **chorizo, or any spicy sausage**, thinly sliced

12 **mussels** on their half shells

12 large **prawns**, shelled and cleaned

olive or sesame oil

25 g (1 oz) **fresh root ginger**, peeled and cut into fine strips

1 large **garlic clove**, chopped

3 tablespoons **salted black beans**

1 tablespoon **lemon juice**

2 tablespoons **soy sauce**

2 teaspoons **sugar**

150 ml (¼ pint) **sherry**

4 x 175 g (6 oz) skinned **white fish** fillets (for example, cod or haddock)

4 large **spring onions**, finely sliced diagonally, plus extra to sprinkle

PREP

15

COOK

25

SERVES

4

spicy

yum!

cool

fish with black bean sauce

Black bean sauce is a traditional accompaniment to fish and chicken in Oriental cooking. It's rich, tasty sauce really livens up a dish.

1 Heat a little oil in a wok or large frying pan and add the ginger, garlic and black beans. Stir-fry for 2 minutes, then stir in the lemon juice, soy sauce, sugar and sherry.

2 Add the fish to the wok. Simmer for 20–25 minutes to cook the fish. Sprinkle the spring onions over the top, cook for 1–2 minutes, then dish up the fish and sauce straight away on a bed of noodles.

salmon fish cakes

Salmon fish cakes make a great starter if you are planning on cooking a celebratory meal. Mix some mayo with lemon juice for a nice tangy dip and dish up with a green salad. For a main course, serve with chips as well.

1 Boil the potatoes in their skins, leave to cool, then peel. Mash in a bowl with the butter or margarine, then mix in the salmon, parsley, a dash of salt and pepper and half the beaten egg. Cover and put in the fridge for 20 minutes.

2 Divide the salmon mix into 8 burgers. Dip each one into the rest of the beaten egg, then into the breadcrumbs until well covered.

3 Heat the oil in a frying pan, add the fish cakes and fry for 2–3 minutes on each side, or until golden brown. Eat immediately with chips or a healthy green salad.

*Plus 20 minutes marinating

PREP

30*

COOK

12

SERVES

4

snack

posh

fresh

300 g (10 oz) **potatoes**

25 g (1 oz) **butter or margarine**

300 g (10 oz) **fresh salmon, cooked, or canned salmon**

2 tablespoons **parsley**, chopped

salt and **pepper**

2 **eggs**, beaten

75 g (3 oz) **breadcrumbs**

oil, for frying

2 pieces of **cod**, about 175 g (6 oz) each

3 tablespoons **breadcrumbs**

3 tablespoons **basil leaves**, torn

3 tablespoons **Parmesan cheese**, grated

2 pieces **sun-dried tomato**, drained and chopped

1 tablespoon **olive oil**

grated rind of ½ **lemon**

salt and **pepper**

fresh

telly

posh

crispy crumbed cod

If you are fed up with greasy fish and chips from the take-away then why not make your own fancy version? You can use any firm white fish such as cod or halibut – whatever you like and is cheapest.

1 Heat the oven to 190°C (375°F), Gas Mark 5.

2 Rinse and dry the pieces of cod and put them into a shallow ovenproof dish.

3 Mix together the breadcrumbs, basil, cheese, tomato, oil and lemon rind and add a sprinkling of salt and pepper. Spoon the topping over the cod and squash into an even layer.

4 Cook in the oven for 20 minutes until the topping is crisp, then dish up with new potatoes and green beans.

creamy fish pie

This light and creamy salmon and cod pie is topped with a delicious lemon and leek mash – comfort food at its best.

PREP

25

COOK

60

SERVES

2

share

yum!

easy

500 g (1 lb) **potatoes**, cut into large chunks

1 small **leek**, cut into cubes

1 large piece of **salmon**, about 250 g (8 oz)

1 piece of **cod**, about 200 g (7 oz)

300 ml (½ pint) **milk**

50 g (2 oz) **butter**

25 g (1 oz) **plain flour**

grated rind and juice of ½ **lemon**

2 tablespoons **parsley**, chopped

salt and **pepper**

1 Boil the potatoes for 15 minutes, until soft, then boil the leeks for 5 minutes, until tender.

2 Meanwhile, put the salmon and cod into a saucepan with the milk. Bring to the boil, reduce the heat and simmer for 5 minutes. Remove and leave to cool for a few minutes.

3 Lift the fish out of the milk, peel off the skin and flake into large pieces, making sure there are no bones, then put on a plate. Keep the milk.

4 Heat the oven to 200°C (400°F), Gas Mark 6.

5 Melt half the butter and stir in the flour. Slowly add the milk and boil, stirring until thick and smooth. Add the lemon rind, parsley and salt and pepper, then stir in the fish. Tip into an ovenproof dish.

6 Drain and mash the potatoes, then beat in the leek, lemon juice, salt and pepper. Spoon the mash over the fish, fluff up the top with a fork and dot over the rest of the butter.

7 Cook in the oven for 25 minutes until the top is golden. Serve with green vegetables.

4 **ready-to-cook pizza bases**

olive oil, for brushing and drizzling

salt and **pepper**

2 **onions**, finely sliced

2 **garlic cloves**, sliced

4 **tomatoes**, skinned and sliced

250 g (8 oz) **spinach**, cooked and chopped

8 slices **Parma ham**, cut into strips

1 tablespoon **black olives**, pitted and chopped

4 **eggs**

PREP

25

COOK

15

SERVES

4

cool

yum!

fun

spinach, parma ham and egg pizza

This is one posh pizza! You can get away with using ham or cooked bacon instead of Parma ham, but if you're trying to impress a date then splash out and get the proper stuff.

1 Heat the oven to 230°C (450°F), Gas Mark 8.

2 Put the pizza bases onto baking sheets. Brush lightly with olive oil and sprinkle with salt and pepper.

3 Mix together the onions, garlic, tomatoes, spinach, Parma ham and olives and spread over the bases, making a hole in the middle of each topping for the egg.

4 Drizzle the pizzas with olive oil and sprinkle with salt and pepper. Cook for 10 minutes, then take the pizzas out of the oven and crack the eggs into the holes. Cook for another 3–5 minutes then eat straight away.

red wine risotto

This is perfect winter comfort food – but with a touch of class. What more can you want? Serve it with a mixed leaf salad and some more red wine.

1 Heat the red wine in a large saucepan to a gentle simmer. Add the stock.

2 Melt half the butter with the oil in another saucepan. Add the garlic and onions and fry gently for 5 minutes, until soft.

3 Add the rice and stir well so it is covered with the butter and oil. Add the hot stock mixture, a large glug at a time, stirring until each addition is absorbed into the rice. Carry on adding the stock in this way, cooking until the rice is creamy but still firm, which should take about 20 minutes. When half the stock has been absorbed, add the mushrooms and a good dash of salt and pepper.

4 When all the stock has been added and the rice is just cooked, add most of the Parmesan and the rest of the butter. Mix well, cover and leave for a few minutes, then sprinkle what is left of the grated Parmesan over the top and dish up. Delicious!

PREP

10

COOK

25

SERVES

4

450 ml (¾ pint) **red wine**

600 ml (1 pint) hot **chicken stock**

125 g (4 oz) **butter**

1 tablespoon **vegetable oil**

2 **garlic cloves**, finely chopped

2 **onions**, finely chopped

300 g (10 oz) **risotto rice**

250 g (8 oz) **mushrooms**, sliced

salt and **pepper**

175 g (6 oz) **Parmesan cheese**, grated

sexy

posh

boozy

125 g (4 oz) **butter**

6 **spring onions or shallots**, finely chopped

150 ml (¼ pint) **white wine**

finely grated rind and juice of 1 **lemon**

500 g (1 lb) **risotto rice**

1.5 litres (2½ pints) hot **chicken or vegetable stock**

salt and **pepper**

2 tablespoons **vodka**

1 tablespoon **thyme**, chopped

75 g (3 oz) **Parmesan cheese**, grated

PREP

COOK

SERVES

lemon and thyme risotto with vodka

Wonderfully light, fragrant and creamy, this really is a sexy dish with a kick!

1 Melt half the butter in a large saucepan, chuck in the spring onions or shallots and fry for 5 minutes, until soft. Pour in the wine, add half the lemon rind, bring to the boil and cook, stirring constantly, until most of the liquid has evaporated.

2 Add the rice and stir well so it is covered with the butter and oil. Add the hot stock mixture, a large glug at a time, stirring until each addition is absorbed into the rice. Carry on adding the stock in this way, cooking until the rice is creamy but still firm, which should take about 20 minutes. When half the stock has been absorbed, add the rest of the butter, the remaining lemon rind and all the juice, vodka, thyme and Parmesan.

3 Cover the pan and leave the risotto for a few minutes, then dish up.

boozy

party

posh

baked bean cassoulet

A great way to liven up the humble old favourite – baked beans.

share

yum!

easy

4 tablespoons **vegetable oil**

4 skinless **chicken thighs or drumsticks**

500 g (1 lb) **herby sausages**

50 g (2 oz) **chorizo or pepperoni sausage**, thinly sliced

2 **onions**, thinly sliced

150 ml (¼ pint) **chicken stock**

3 **garlic cloves**, crushed

several **sprigs of thyme**

2 x 415 g (13½ oz) **cans baked beans**

2 tablespoons **Worcestershire sauce**

2 tablespoons **tomato purée**

salt and **pepper**

75 g (3 oz) **breadcrumbs**

1 Heat the oven to 180°C (350°F), Gas Mark 4.

2 Heat the oil in a large frying pan and fry the chicken pieces and sausages for about 10 minutes until golden. Add the chorizo or pepperoni and onions and fry for another 2 minutes.

3 Put in an ovenproof dish and add the stock, garlic and thyme. Stir well, cover then bake in the oven for 30 minutes.

4 Stir in the baked beans, Worcestershire sauce, tomato purée, salt and pepper, and mix again. Sprinkle the breadcrumbs over the top and put back in the oven, uncovered, for 25–30 minutes until the breadcrumbs are golden and the chicken is cooked. Dish up straight away.

spicy tortillas

PREP

20

COOK

50

SERVES

4

1 tablespoon **olive oil**

500 g (1 lb) **beef mince**

1 **onion**, chopped

2 **carrots**, chopped

2 **garlic cloves**, crushed

2 teaspoons mild **paprika**

1 teaspoon **ground cumin**

415 g (13½ oz) **can baked beans**

400 g (13 oz) **can chopped tomatoes**

200 ml (7 fl oz) **chicken or beef stock**

salt and **pepper**

Topping:

125 g (4 oz) **frozen mixed vegetables**

125 g (4 oz) original **tortilla chips**

75 g (3 oz) **Cheddar or mozzarella cheese**, grated

Hire a video, curl up on the sofa, and enjoy the ultimate TV meal – spicy beef and beans with a vegetable and tortilla chip topping.

1 Heat the oil in a saucepan and add the mince, onion, carrots and garlic. Fry, stirring, until the mince is brown all over.

2 Stir in the paprika and cumin and cook for 1 minute. Add the baked beans, tomatoes, stock, and a dash of salt and pepper. Bring to the boil, stirring, then cover and simmer for 45 minutes, stirring from time to time so it doesn't stick.

3 Boil the frozen vegetables according to the packet instructions, then drain.

4 Pour the mince into a shallow ovenproof dish. Chuck the vegetables over the mince, top with the tortilla chips and then sprinkle with cheese. Grill for a few minutes until the cheese is bubbling. Gorgeous!

cool

telly

easy

chilli chips

PREP

5

COOK

55

SERVES

4

snack

mates

spicy

4 large **potatoes**

4–6 tablespoons **olive oil**

½ teaspoon **salt**

1–2 teaspoons **chilli powder**

Use as little or as much chilli powder as you like. Just make sure you have a cold lager to wash down these spicy chips.

1 Heat the oven to 220°C (425°F), Gas Mark 7.

2 Chop each potato into 8 wedges and put in a bowl. Add the olive oil, salt and chilli powder and toss well.

3 Put on a baking sheet and cook in the oven for 15 minutes. Turn over and cook for another 15 minutes, then turn once more and cook for a final 25–30 minutes until crisp and golden. These make a great snack with soured cream, mayonnaise or aïoli.

375 g (12 oz) **tagliatelle**

1 tablespoon **vegetable oil**

1 **yellow pepper**, cored, deseeded and chopped

2 **garlic cloves**, crushed

125 g (4 oz) **mushrooms**, sliced

125 g (4 oz) **rindless bacon**, grilled and cut into thin strips

1 tablespoon chopped **parsley**

pepper

500 g (1 lb) **fromage frais or natural yogurt**

25 g (1 oz) **pine nuts**, toasted

mates

easy

snack

tagliatelle with bacon and mushrooms

Pasta is so versatile, and the smoky bacon along with the crunchy pine nuts make a lively yet creamy sauce. One to cook when your parents come to visit ...

1 Cook the tagliatelle according to the packet instructions.

2 Meanwhile, heat the oil in a frying pan, add the chopped yellow pepper and fry for 2–3 minutes. Stir in the garlic, mushrooms, bacon, parsley and a dash of pepper.

3 Turn down the heat and stir in the fromage frais or yogurt. Stir and heat gently.

4 Drain the pasta and toss with the sauce, then sprinkle with the pine nuts. Dish up with an Italian-style salad and fresh ciabatta bread.

easy roast chicken

A whole roast chicken can be too much for just two people, so why not buy a couple of joints instead? They will taste just as good and take less time to cook.

1 Heat the oven to 200°C (400°F), Gas Mark 6.

2 Make 2 slits in each chicken breast and put a bay leaf in each cut. Cut 2 slices of orange, halve each slice and slide a piece under each bay leaf. Put the chicken into a large roasting tin and squeeze the juice from the rest of the orange over it.

3 Put the vegetables and garlic around the chicken, drizzle over the oil and sprinkle with salt and pepper.

4 Roast in the oven for 50 minutes, turning once or twice and basting in the juices from time to time. Drizzle with honey and cook for another 10 minutes or until the chicken juices are clear when you stick a knife into the thickest part of the breasts, and the vegetables are golden.

5 To make the gravy, mix the cornflour and mustard with a little cold stock. Stir in the rest of the stock and a dash of salt and pepper.

6 Pour the stock into the roasting tin with the pan juices, bring to the boil and boil, stirring, until thick and smooth. Sublime!

PREP

20

COOK

60

SERVES

2

yum!

party

juicy

2 large **chicken breasts**, on the bone

4 **bay leaves**

1 **orange**

200 g (7 oz) **shallots**

200 g (7 oz) **parsnips**, cut into chunks

200 g (7 oz) **carrots**, cut into chunks

400 g (13 oz) **new potatoes**, halved if large

6 **garlic cloves**, unpeeled

3 tablespoons **olive oil**

salt and **pepper**

3 teaspoons **honey**

Gravy:

2 teaspoons **cornflour**

1 teaspoon **mustard**

250 ml (8 fl oz) **chicken stock**

salt and **pepper**

5 kg (10 lb) **turkey**

1 packet **ready-made stuffing**

1 tablespoon **dried basil**

salt and **pepper**

600 ml (1 pint) **chicken or vegetable stock**

6 tablespoons **port**

1 tablespoon **cornflour**

45

200

SERVES

8

juicy

mates

party

traditional roast turkey

Why not wow your mates at Christmas or Thanksgiving with a turkey roast. It may sound rather daunting, but don't be put off, as it's really quite straightforward. Keep it simple the first time and serve with mashed potatoes and vegetables.

1 Heat the oven to 180°C (350°F), Gas Mark 4.

2 Put the turkey into a large roasting tin and stuff the neck with the stuffing. Sprinkle with basil and salt and pepper and roast in the oven for 15–20 minutes per 500 g (1 lb), plus 20 minutes extra. Baste regularly.

3 Remove the foil 20 minutes before the end so the turkey browns, and pour off the pan juices into a saucepan to make the gravy.

4 Skim off the fat and boil up the juices with the stock and the port. Slowly stir in cornflour mixed with a little cold water to thicken the gravy. Then carve the turkey and eat with mashed potatoes, carrots and green beans.

roast lamb with rosemary

PREP

5

COOK

120

SERVES

6

This lovely dish has so much flavour, texture and attitude. Why save it for a Sunday?

1.5 kg (3 lb) **leg of lamb**

2–4 **garlic cloves**, sliced

3–4 **rosemary sprigs**

salt and **pepper**

1 tablespoon **vegetable oil**

150 ml (¼ pint) **white wine or vegetable stock**

1 Heat the oven to 180°C (350°F), Gas Mark 4.

2 Make small cuts into the lamb and put a piece of garlic and a few rosemary leaves into each cut. Sprinkle with salt and pepper and put in a roasting tin. Drizzle with the oil.

3 Cook in the oven for about 2 hours, then put on a plate and cover with foil while you make the gravy.

4 Skim the fat off the juices in the pan, pour in the wine or stock and bring to the boil, stirring, until thick. Add salt and pepper if it needs it.

5 Carve the meat, dish up with vegetables and roast potatoes and add a good glug of gravy on top.

share

posh

fab

1 kg (2 lb) **joint of beef** for roasting

mustard

pepper

Yorkshire puddings:

125 g (4 oz) **plain flour**

pinch of **salt**

1 large **egg**

300 ml (½ pint) **milk**, or **milk mixed with water**

margarine or vegetable oil for greasing

PREP

20

COOK

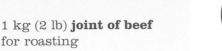
60

SERVES

6

juicy

beer

mates

roast beef with individual yorkshire puds

What a lunch! If you aren't feeling brave then you can always buy frozen Yorkshire puddings instead of making your own.

1 Heat the oven to 220°C (425°F), Gas Mark 7.

2 Put the meat in a roasting tin and sprinkle with pepper. Thinly spread with mustard.

3 Roast in the oven for 15 minutes per 500 g (1 lb) plus 15 minutes for rare beef; 20 minutes per 500 g (1 lb) plus 20 minutes for medium-cooked beef; 25 minutes per 500 g (1 lb) plus 25 minutes for well-cooked beef. Turn the heat down to 190°C (375°F), Gas Mark 5 after the first hour.

4 Meanwhile, make the Yorkshire puddings. Mix the flour, salt, egg and milk or milk and water to make a batter.

5 Take the beef out of the oven and turn up the heat to 230° C (450°F), Gas Mark 8.

6 Grease 6 muffin tins, heat them up, whisk the batter and then pour the batter in. Cook for 10–12 minutes until well risen. Turn down the heat to 220°C (425°F), Gas Mark 7 and put the meat back in the oven. Cook for 8–15 minutes then take out the meat and Yorkshire puddings and dish up with vegetables and gravy.

roast spuds and parsnips

Irresistibly crunchy, no roast dinner is complete without them! They're not difficult to make – just make sure you get them in the oven 45 minutes before the roast lamb, chicken or turkey is ready.

1 Place the potatoes and parsnips in a pan of boiling salted water and parboil for 5 minutes, then drain.

2 Put the potatoes and parsnips into a roasting tin and drizzle the oil over. Turn the parsnips so that they are well coated with the oil. Sprinkle some salt and pepper on and cook in a preheated oven, 180°C (350°F), Gas Mark 4, for 45 minutes until tender, basting with the oil occasionally.

PREP

10

COOK

45

SERVES

6

yum!

share

easy

1 kg (2 lb) **potatoes**, peeled and quartered

750 g (1½ lb) **parsnips**, trimmed and quartered lengthways

4 tablespoons **vegetable** or **sunflower oil**

salt and **pepper**

east is east

750 g (1½ lb) boneless, skinless **chicken breasts**, cut into cubes

6 tablespoons **ready-made tikka curry paste**

75 g (3 oz) **natural yogurt**

1 tablespoon **vegetable oil**

Masala sauce:

4 tablespoons **ghee**

2 tablespoons **ready-made curry paste**, for medium-hot curry

1 tablespoon **tandoori paste**

2 teaspoons **tomato purée**

2 **tomatoes**, skinned and chopped

1 **red pepper**, cored, deseeded and chopped

1 tablespoon **coriander leaves**, chopped

1 tablespoon **ground almonds**

2 tablespoons **single cream**

pinch of **sugar**

salt

COOK

25

SERVES

4

mates

beer

spicy

chicken tikka masala

You can also make this delicious Indian speciality with fish rather than chicken – just make sure you choose firm white fish like cod or haddock.

1 Mix the curry paste with the yogurt and oil, then coat the chicken with it. Cover and put in the fridge for at least 6 hours, or overnight. Put 2 tablespoons of the marinade in a bowl to use later.

2 Take the pieces of chicken out of the marinade and spear onto skewers. Grill for 10–15 minutes, turning 2 or 3 times.

3 Meanwhile, make the masala sauce. Heat the ghee in a frying pan. Fry the curry paste for 5 minutes. Add the tandoori paste and the 2 tablespoons of extra marinade and fry for 2 minutes. Add the tomato purée, tomatoes and red pepper and simmer. Add a little water to make a creamy sauce, plus the coriander, almonds, cream and sugar and a dash of salt.

4 When the tikkas are cooked, take them off the skewers and stir into the sauce. Eat with rice and naan bread.

*Plus at least 6 hours marinating

thai green curry with chicken

Green curries are spicy yet soothing due to the great mix of chilli and creamy coconut milk. This is so luscious that you won't be able to resist eating it all!

1 Heat the oil in a wok or large frying pan, toss in the ginger and shallots and fry over a gentle heat, stirring for about 3 minutes or until soft. Add the green curry paste and fry for another 2 minutes.

2 Add the chicken to the wok or frying pan, stir well and fry for 3 minutes. Stir in the coconut milk, bring to the boil, then turn down the heat and cook the curry gently, stirring occasionally, for 10 minutes or until the chicken is cooked and the sauce is thick.

3 Stir in the fish sauce, sugar, lime leaves and chilli and cook the curry for another 5 minutes. Taste and add salt and pepper if it needs it, then dish up on a bed of rice.

PREP

10

COOK

25

SERVES

4

share

juicy

fab

2 tablespoons **vegetable oil**

2.5 cm (1 inch) piece of **fresh root ginger**, peeled and finely chopped

1 **small onion or** 2 **shallots**, chopped

4 tablespoons **Thai green curry paste**

625 g (1¼ lb) boneless, skinless **chicken thighs**, cut into chunks

300 ml (½ pint) **coconut milk**

4 teaspoons **Thai fish sauce**

1 teaspoon **sugar**

3 **kaffir lime leaves**, shredded

1 **green chilli**, deseeded and sliced

salt and **pepper**

1 teaspoon **vegetable oil**

500 g (1 lb) boneless, skinless **chicken breasts**, cut into thin strips

125 g (4 oz) **white cabbage**, finely shredded

125 g (4 oz) **bean sprouts**

1 large **green pepper**, cored, deseeded and cut lengthways into thin strips

2 **carrots**, about 250 g (8 oz), cut lengthways into thin strips

2 **garlic cloves**, crushed

pepper

Sauce:

2 teaspoons **cornflour**

4 tablespoons **water**

3 tablespoons **soy sauce**

PREP

15

COOK

10

SERVES

4

fast

fresh

cool

stir-fried chicken and vegetables

The secrets of a successful stir-fry are to have a large enough pan, to make sure the oil is really hot before you add anything, and to ensure that everything is chopped and ready to toss in so that nothing overcooks.

1 Make the sauce: mix the cornflour with the water to make a paste, then stir in the soy sauce.

2 Heat the oil in a wok or large frying pan until really hot. Add the chicken strips and stir-fry for 3–4 minutes or until coloured all over. Then take them out of the pan and put on a plate.

3 Reheat the wok or frying pan over a medium heat then add the vegetables and garlic and stir-fry for 2–3 minutes or until the green pepper is just starting to go soft.

4 Stir the sauce, then pour into the wok or frying pan. Turn up the heat to high and toss the ingredients until the sauce is thick and covers all the vegetables. Add the chicken and its juices and toss for 1–2 minutes until all the ingredients are mixed together. Sprinkle with pepper then eat straight away. Lovely!

chicken and cashew stir-fry

Once you get the hang of stir-fries then you can add any vegetables or meat you like. Cooking really isn't mysterious, so get out there and experiment!

1 Heat the oil in a wok or large frying pan and add the chicken, onion, baby sweetcorn and cashew nuts. Stir-fry over a high heat for 3 minutes.

2 Turn down the heat and stir in the soy sauce. Then add the stock, sugar, spring onion and a dash of pepper. Turn up the heat and stir-fry for another 2 minutes.

3 Dish up, sprinkle with chilli, and get the chopsticks ready.

PREP

6

COOK

5

SERVES

2

easy

juicy

yum!

3 tablespoons **vegetable oil**

250 g (8 oz) skinless, boneless **chicken**, cut into bite-sized pieces

½ **onion**, sliced

50 g (2 oz) **baby sweetcorn**, sliced diagonally

50 g (2 oz) **cashew nuts**

125 ml (4 fl oz) **soy sauce**

4 tablespoons **chicken stock**

4 teaspoons **brown sugar**

15 g (½ oz) **spring onion**, sliced diagonally

pepper

1 large **red chilli**, sliced diagonally, to top

balti chicken

6 tablespoons **vegetable oil**

1 **onion**, chopped

½ teaspoon **turmeric**

1 teaspoon **ground coriander**

1 teaspoon **ground cumin**

1 teaspoon **chilli powder**

2 tablespoons **water**

750 g (1½ lb) boneless, skinless **chicken**, cut into cubes

1 kg (2 lb) **tomatoes**, chopped

salt

1 **green pepper**, cored, deseeded and chopped

½ teaspoon chopped **garlic cloves**

2 **green chillies**, chopped

PREP

20

COOK

30

SERVES

4

spicy

beer

party

A deliciously spicy meal that transforms chicken with a fab mix of Indian herbs. Have it with naan bread and rice or salad.

1 Heat the oil in a wok or large frying pan, add the onion and fry until soft.

2 Mix the turmeric, coriander, cumin and chilli powder in a bowl with the water. Stir into the onion and simmer until the liquid has dried up – about 3–4 minutes. Add the chicken and fry on all sides, then add the tomatoes and a pinch of salt. Cover and cook for 15 minutes.

3 Add the green pepper, garlic and chillies. Cook, uncovered, until all the tomato juices have evaporated and the chicken is cooked. Eat with naan bread and rice and a salad.

turkey and orange stir-fry

PREP

30*

COOK

10

SERVES

4

The orange juice gives this crisp dish a really great citrus zing, and makes it rather unusual. One to try!

1 First make the marinade. Mix the soy sauce and orange juice then put the turkey into the marinade and leave for 30 minutes.

2 Mix the orange juice with enough water to make 150 ml (¼ pint). Mix in the cornflour and a dash of salt and pepper.

3 Take the turkey out of the marinade and put on a plate. Keep the marinade.

4 Heat the oil in a wok or large frying pan. Add the turkey and stir-fry for 4–5 minutes, then add the orange rind, peppers, celery and carrots. Stir-fry for another 3 minutes.

5 Pour in the cornflour mixture and the marinade. Bring to the boil and stir well until it starts to thicken, then dish up on a mound of boiled rice.

*Plus 30 minutes marinating

mates

fruity

posh

375 g (12 oz) skinless **turkey breast fillets**, cut into large chunks

grated rind and juice of 2 **oranges**

1 tablespoon **cornflour**

salt and **pepper**

1 tablespoon **vegetable oil**

½ **red pepper**, cored, deseeded and cut into strips

½ **green pepper**, cored, deseeded and cut into strips

3 **celery sticks**, cut into cubes

125 g (4 oz) **carrots**, cut into thin slices

Marinade:

1 tablespoon **soy sauce**

2 tablespoons **orange juice**

½ teaspoon **saffron threads**

750 g (1½ lb) boneless **leg of lamb**, cut into cubes

150 g (5 oz) **natural yogurt**

1 teaspoon **salt**

2 tablespoons **ghee**

¼ teaspoon ground **cardamom**

½ teaspoon **cinnamon**

1½ teaspoons **ground cumin**

300 ml (½ pint) **coconut milk**

3 tablespoons chopped **coriander leaves**

Curry paste:

2 **onions**, finely chopped

3 **garlic cloves**, chopped

2.5 cm (1 inch) piece **fresh root ginger**, peeled and chopped

2 **green chillies**, de-seeded and chopped

50 g (2 oz) **ground almonds**

150 ml (¼ pint) **water**

COOK

60

SERVES

4

mates

spicy

beer

lamb korma

This favourite mild lamb curry is cooked with yogurt, coconut milk, saffron, ginger and ground almonds. Such a good curry only needs a cold beer, and you have perfection.

1 Infuse the saffron threads in 2 tablespoons of boiling water for 10 minutes.

2 Put the lamb in a bowl. Mix together the yogurt, saffron and its water and the salt. Pour over the lamb, cover and leave to marinate for 2 hours.

3 Put the ingredients for the paste into a bowl and mash really well until smooth.

4 Heat the ghee in a frying pan, add the cardamom, cinnamon, cumin and fry over a low heat for 1 minute. Stir in the paste and cook, stirring frequently, for another 5 minutes.

5 Add the coconut milk and the lamb and saffron yogurt, bring to the boil, then turn down the heat. Cover and cook very gently, stirring occasionally, for 45 minutes, or until the lamb is tender and the sauce is thick.

6 Stir in 2 tablespoons of the coriander leaves and dish up with the rest of the coriander scattered over the top.

*Plus 2 hours marinating

stir-fried beef with baby sweetcorn

This may seem like a luxury dish as it uses steak, but it's worth spending the extra as it's so delicious that it will become a real favourite when you need a treat.

PREP

25

COOK

10

SERVES

4

easy

fast

fresh

1 First make the sauce. Put all the ingredients in a bowl or jug and mix well.

2 Heat 2 tablespoons of the vegetable oil in a wok or large frying pan until really hot. Add the beef, chillies and a good sprinkling of pepper and stir-fry for 3–4 minutes until the beef is brown all over. Tip it all into a bowl.

3 Add the rest of the oil to the wok or frying pan and heat until hot. Add the onion and red pepper and stir-fry for 2–3 minutes, then add the baby sweetcorn and stir-fry for another couple of minutes.

4 Pour the beef and its juices back into the wok or frying pan together with the sauce. Toss for 2–3 minutes until everything is mixed and hot, then eat straight away.

3 tablespoons **vegetable oil**

500 g (1 lb) **rump or fillet steak**, cut into thin strips

2 **fresh green chillies**, deseeded and finely chopped

pepper

1 **onion**, thinly sliced

1 **red pepper**, cored, deseeded and cut lengthways into thin strips

425 g (14 oz) **can baby sweetcorn**, drained

Sauce:

3 tablespoons **soy sauce**

2 tablespoons **sherry**

1 tablespoon **sugar**

1 teaspoon **five spice powder**

1 tablespoon **vegetable oil**

1 **garlic clove**, finely chopped

500 g (1 lb) **rump or fillet steak**, cut into long, thin strips

1 **lemon grass stalk**, finely chopped

2.5 cm (1 inch) piece of **fresh root ginger**, peeled and finely chopped

1 **red pepper**, cored, deseeded and thickly sliced

1 **green pepper**, cored, deseeded and thickly sliced

1 **onion**, thickly sliced

2 tablespoons **lime juice**

pepper

cool

posh

yum!

thai beef and mixed pepper stir-fry

The deliciously fresh flavours of ginger and lemon grass make this a real winner. Fresh, easy to cook, and incredibly tasty, this is one to cook again and again.

1 Heat the vegetable oil in a wok or large frying pan over a high heat. Add the garlic and stir-fry for 1 minute.

2 Add the beef and stir-fry for 2–3 minutes until slightly coloured. Stir in the lemon grass and ginger then tip the beef into a bowl.

3 Heat the wok or frying pan up again and stir-fry the peppers and onion for 2–3 minutes until the onions are just turning brown and going soft.

4 Chuck the beef back into the pan, stir in the lime juice and sprinkle with pepper. Dish up on a pile of rice or noodles.

vegetable biryani

Clean, fresh and fragrant – very Zen! If you can't cope without meat in your diet then add some cooked chicken at the same time as you add the yogurt.

1 Cook the rice according to the packet instructions and drain.

2 Meanwhile, heat the oil in a saucepan, add the carrots, potato, ginger and garlic and fry for 10 minutes until soft.

3 Stir in the cauliflower, beans, curry paste, turmeric and cinnamon and cook for 1 minute.

4 Stir in the yogurt and raisins. Pile the rice on top of the vegetables, cover and cook over a low heat for 10 minutes, checking it isn't sticking to the pan.

5 Dollop the biryani onto plates, sprinkle the cashew nuts and coriander over the top and tuck in.

PREP

10

COOK

20

SERVES

2

fab

share

beer

250 g (8 oz) **long-grain rice**

1 tablespoon **olive oil**

2 **carrots**, chopped

1 large **potato**, chopped

2.5 cm (1 inch) piece of **fresh root ginger**, peeled and grated

2 **garlic cloves**, crushed

150 g (5 oz) **cauliflower** florets

100 g (3½ oz) **green beans**, cut in half

1 tablespoon **hot curry paste**

1 teaspoon **turmeric**

½ teaspoon **ground cinnamon**

150 g (5 oz) **natural yogurt**

25 g (1 oz) **raisins**

To top:

50 g (2 oz) **cashew nuts**, toasted

2 tablespoons chopped **coriander leaves**

3 tablespoons **vegetable oil**

25 g (1 oz) **flaked almonds**

2 **onions**, sliced

2.5 cm (1 inch) piece **fresh root ginger**, peeled and grated

2 **garlic cloves**, sliced

1 teaspoon **turmeric**

2 teaspoons **medium curry paste**

4 **carrots**, thinly sliced

1 **cauliflower**, cut into florets

450 ml (¾ pint) **vegetable stock**

2 **courgettes**, sliced

125 g (4 oz) **frozen peas**

200 ml (7 fl oz) **coconut milk**

50 g (2 oz) **ground almonds**

3 tablespoons **double cream**

salt and **pepper**

easy

fast

spicy

quick vegetable korma

You can use other vegetables, such as beans, broccoli, mangetout and aubergine in this simple curry, then dish up with poppadums, basmati rice, naan bread and mango chutney for an Indian banquet.

1 Heat the oil in a large saucepan. Toss in the flaked almonds and fry gently for 1–2 minutes until toasted, then put on a plate.

2 Add the onions, ginger, garlic, turmeric and curry paste to the pan. Fry for 5 minutes.

3 Add the carrots and cauliflower and fry for another 5 minutes. Pour in the stock and bring to the boil. Turn down the heat, cover the pan and simmer for 20–25 minutes until the vegetables are tender.

4 Add the courgettes, peas, coconut milk and ground almonds then simmer, uncovered, for 3 minutes. Stir in the cream and a pinch of salt and pepper. Dish up and sprinkle with the flaked almonds.

chickpea and potato curry

If you fancy something spicy, healthy and fast then this is perfect! It is delicious simply with basmati rice, naan or plenty of grainy bread, plus your favourite type of chutney and a salad.

1 Heat the oil in a large saucepan. Add the onion, turmeric, curry paste and potato and fry gently for 5 minutes.

2 Add the chickpeas, tomatoes, sugar and a little salt and pepper. Bring to the boil, then turn down the heat and cook, uncovered, for about 20 minutes, stirring lots and breaking up the tomatoes.

3 Stir in the chopped coriander and add more salt and pepper if it needs it, then dip in some bread and tuck in.

PREP

10

COOK

25

SERVES

2

cool

cheap

share

2 tablespoons **vegetable oil**

1 large **onion**, chopped

1 teaspoon **turmeric**

2 teaspoons **medium curry paste**

1 large **potato**, cut into cubes

400 g (13 oz) can **chickpeas**, drained and rinsed

800 g (1 lb 10 oz) **can plum tomatoes**

2 teaspoons **sugar**

salt and **pepper**

small handful of **coriander leaves**, chopped

vegetable oil, for deep-frying

250 g (8 oz) **tofu**, cut into cubes

75 g (3 oz) **egg noodles**

125 g (4 oz) **broccoli** florets

125 g (4 oz) **baby sweetcorn**, cut in half

3 tablespoons **soy sauce**

1 tablespoon **lemon juice**

1 teaspoon **sugar**

1 teaspoon **chilli sauce**

1 **garlic clove**, chopped

1 **red chilli**, deseeded and sliced

2 **eggs**, lightly beaten

125 g (4 oz) drained **water chestnuts**, sliced

PREP

20

COOK

15

SERVES

4

fab

easy

fresh

egg-fried noodles with tofu

Tofu is a great source of protein, and when it takes on all these other lovely flavours it makes a really good tasty, healthy dish.

1 In a saucepan, heat about 5 cm (2 inches) of vegetable oil (check it's hot enough by dropping in a cube of bread which should brown in 30 seconds). Add the tofu and fry for 3–4 minutes until crisp and golden. Drain on kitchen paper.

2 Cook the noodles according to the packet instructions, drain, plunge under cold water and dry well on kitchen paper.

3 Boil the broccoli and sweetcorn for 1 minute, drain, plunge under cold water and pat dry with kitchen paper.

4 Mix together the soy sauce, lemon juice, sugar and chilli sauce.

5 Heat 3 tablespoons of vegetable oil in a wok or large frying pan, add the garlic and chilli and stir-fry for 3 minutes. Add the noodles and stir-fry for 5 minutes until starting to crisp up.

6 Stir in the eggs, and stir-fry for 1 minute, then stir in the sauce mixture, tofu, broccoli, sweetcorn and water chestnuts and stir-fry for another 2–3 minutes, then dish up. Fab!

chow mein

Make sure the wok or frying pan is very hot before adding any ingredients, and keep tossing everything around from the middle to the sides so it cooks evenly.

250 g (8 oz) **rice noodles**

2 tablespoons **vegetable oil**

3-4 **spring onions**, sliced thinly diagonally

2.5 cm (1 inch) piece of **fresh root ginger**, peeled and finely chopped

1 **garlic clove**, crushed

2 skinless, boneless **chicken breasts**, cut into thin strips

125 g (4 oz) **mangetout**

125 g (4 oz) **cooked ham**, shredded

75 g (3 oz) **bean sprouts**

pepper

1 Cook the rice noodles according to the packet instructions.

2 Meanwhile, make the sauce. Mix the cornflour with 2 tablespoons of stock or water to make a smooth paste, then stir in the rest of the stock or water, the soy sauce, sherry and sesame oil.

3 Drain the noodles, plunge under cold water and drain again.

yum!

4 Heat the oil in a wok or large frying pan over a medium heat, chuck in the spring onions, ginger and garlic and stir-fry for 1–2 minutes until soft but not brown. Add the chicken, turn the heat up to high and stir-fry for 3-4 minutes until lightly coloured all over.

sexy

5 Add the mangetout to the pan and stir-fry for 1–2 minutes, then add the ham and bean sprouts and stir-fry to mix.

6 Stir the sauce, pour into the wok and bring to the boil, stirring all the time. Add the noodles and a pinch of pepper and toss until completely mixed and everything is hot. Lovely!

cool

Sauce:

2 teaspoons **cornflour**

8 tablespoons **chicken stock or water**

2 tablespoons **soy sauce**

2 tablespoons **dry sherry**

2 teaspoons **sesame oil**

125 g (4 oz) **broccoli** florets

125 g (4 oz) **green beans**, cut into 2.5 cm (1 inch) lengths

1 **red pepper**, cored, deseeded and sliced

125 g (4 oz) **courgettes**, thinly sliced

Coconut sauce:

25 g (1 oz) **tamarind pulp**

150 ml (¼ pint) **boiling water**

425 g (14 oz) **coconut milk**

2 teaspoons **Thai green curry paste**

1 teaspoon grated **fresh root ginger**

1 **onion**, cut into small cubes

½ teaspoon **turmeric**

salt

posh

fruity

fresh

vegetables in malaysian coconut sauce

You can buy tamarind pulp from large supermarkets and Asian food stores, and it's worth trying to get it as its sweet and sour flavour adds a delicious bite. If you can't find it then use lemon juice or vinegar instead.

1 First make the coconut sauce. Put the tamarind into a bowl. Pour over the boiling water and leave to soak for 30 minutes. Mash the tamarind in the water, then sieve, squashing the tamarind so you get as much of the pulp as possible.

2 Take 2 tablespoons of the cream from the top of the coconut milk and pour it into a wok or large frying pan. Add the curry paste, ginger, onion and turmeric and cook over a gentle heat, stirring, for 2–3 minutes. Stir in the rest of the coconut milk and the tamarind water. Bring to the boil, then turn down the heat and add a dash of salt.

3 Add the broccoli to the sauce and cook for 5 minutes, then add the green beans and red pepper, and cook, stirring, for another 5 minutes. Finally, stir in the courgettes and cook for 1–2 minutes. Dish up and eat with some crispy prawn crackers.

*Plus 30 minutes soaking

lentil, aubergine and coconut dhal

The creamy, mildly spiced dhal makes a delicious accompaniment to Indian curries.

share

beer

juicy

1 Put the lentils in a saucepan with the turmeric, cinnamon sticks and vegetable stock. Bring to the boil, cover and simmer for 35–40 minutes until the lentils are soft and most of the stock has been absorbed.

2 Meanwhile, heat 1 tablespoon of the oil in a frying pan. Add the chillies, garlic, fenugreek seeds and mustard seeds and fry for 5 minutes until golden. Pour into a bowl, putting a teaspoon of the spice mix to one side.

3 Add the rest of the oil to the frying pan and fry the onion and aubergine for 10 minutes until golden. Pour the chilli mixture into the pan and add the garam masala, lentils, tomato purée and lemon juice. Simmer for 5 minutes.

4 Meanwhile, mix together the yogurt, 2 tablespoons of the fresh coriander and 1 teaspoon of spice mixture to make the topping.

5 Stir the creamed coconut into the dhal until melted and add the rest of the coriander. Sprinkle with salt and pepper and dish up with a dollop of the yogurt mix on top.

175 g (6 oz) **split red lentils**, rinsed

1 teaspoon **turmeric**

2 **cinnamon sticks**

750 ml (1¼ pints) **hot vegetable stock**

4 tablespoons **vegetable oil**

4 **red chillies**, deseeded and chopped

2 **garlic cloves**, crushed

2 teaspoons **fenugreek seeds**

1 teaspoon **mustard seeds**

1 large **onion**, chopped

1 **aubergine**, cut into cubes

2 teaspoons **garam masala**

2 tablespoons **tomato purée**

1 tablespoon **lemon juice**

50 g (2 oz) **creamed coconut**

3 tablespoons chopped **coriander leaves**

salt and **pepper**

natural yogurt

sweet stuff

fruit crumble

2 large cooking apples

1 **mango**

juice of 1 **lemon**

125–150 g (4–5 oz) **sugar**

200 g (7 oz) **plain flour**

1 teaspoon **baking powder**

75 g (3 oz) **butter**, cut into small pieces

25–50 g (1–2 oz) **porridge oats**

easy

fruity

yum!

A good crumble, with a crunchy top and soft, sweet layer of fruit, makes a great pudding. Apple and mango is an original combination, but apples are also good with raisins or blackberries. Peaches, rhubarb or plums are ideal for crumble, as well. You just need 500 g (1 lb) fruit in total.

1 Heat the oven to 180°C (350°F), Gas Mark 4.

2 Peel, core and slice the apples. Peel and slice the mango, chucking out the stone. Mix the fruit with the lemon juice and 25–50 g (1–2 oz) of the sugar in a buttered 1.8 litre (3 pint) or similar ovenproof dish.

3 Mix the flour and baking powder in a bowl. Add the butter and rub in until the mixture looks like breadcrumbs. Stir in the rest of the sugar, plus the oats.

4 Tip the crumble over the fruit, level it out, and bake in the oven for about 30 minutes, until the top is golden brown. It tastes great served with custard, vanilla ice cream or creamy yogurt.

italian trifle

This is best made the day before so that the yummy flavours blend together. If you can't get hold of blueberries then use raspberries or blackberries instead.

1 Spread the sponge fingers with the blueberry jam and put in a glass bowl. Sprinkle over the sherry or white wine and half of the blueberries.

2 Mix a little milk with the cornflour until smooth. Stir into the rest of the milk. Pour into a saucepan and bring to the boil, stirring all the time as the milk thickens. When it is boiling and smooth take it off the heat.

3 Whisk the egg yolks and sugar in a bowl until they are light and creamy. Add the milk slowly, whisking all the time. Mix well, pour over the blueberries and sponge fingers, then sprinkle the rest of the blueberries over the top. Leave to cool.

4 Softly whip the cream and spread it over the trifle, then sprinkle grated chocolate over the top.

party

cool

share

8 **sponge fingers**

2 tablespoons **blueberry jam**

50 ml (2 fl oz) **sweet sherry or sweet white wine**

250 g (8 oz) **blueberries**

300 ml (½ pint) **milk**

1 tablespoon **cornflour**

2 **egg yolks**

2 tablespoons **sugar**

300 ml (½ pint) **whipping cream**

50 g (2 oz) **chocolate**, grated

4 tablespoons **double cream**, plus extra to top

50 g (2 oz) **butter**

4 tablespoons **brown sugar**

Sponge:

25 g (1 oz) **walnuts**, finely chopped

125 (4 oz) **butter**, softened

125 g (4 oz) **brown sugar**

2 **eggs**

75 g (3 oz) **self-raising flour**

yum!

gooey

party

sticky toffee puddings

This is one of those fantastic puddings that has a sticky sponge base with luscious gooey sauce on top, but is surprisingly quick to prepare and cook. One to make you smile!

1 Heat the oven to 190°C (375°F), Gas Mark 5.

2 Mix 4 tablespoons of the cream, the butter and the sugar together and divide between 4 small dishes or ramekins.

3 To make the sponge, beat the walnuts, butter, sugar, eggs and flour together until really smooth. Dollop over the toffee mixture in each dish and level off.

4 Bake in the oven for 20–25 minutes until the puddings have risen and are turning golden.

5 Meanwhile, lightly whisk the rest of the cream.

6 Turn the puddings upside-down onto plates, take off the dishes, and add a good dollop of the whisked cream.

banoffi pie

A truly decadent pudding – a crunchy base topped with sweet toffee, bananas, cream and chocolate. Not one for calorie-counters.

1 Crush the digestive biscuits in a clean plastic bag with a rolling pin or wine bottle.

2 Melt the butter in a saucepan and stir in the crumbs. Press the biscuit mix evenly over the base and sides of a deep 20 cm (8 inch) round flat tin or similar. Put in the fridge for an hour.

3 To make the filling, put the butter and sugar in a saucepan over a low heat. Once the butter has melted, stir in the condensed milk and bring slowly to the boil. Turn down the heat and simmer for 5 minutes, stirring all the time, until the mixture goes a caramel colour. Pour onto the biscuit base and chill in the fridge until the mixture has set.

4 Slice the bananas and toss in the lemon juice. Keep a quarter of the bananas for the top and spread the rest over the filling.

5 Whip the cream until thick and dollop over the top. Decorate with the rest of the bananas and sprinkle with the chocolate. Nice one!

*Plus 1 hour chilling

PREP

15*

COOK

10

SERVES
6

fab

posh

sexy

Base:

250 g (8 oz) **digestive biscuits**

125 g (4 oz) **butter**

Filling:

175 g (6 oz) **butter**

175 g (6 oz) **sugar**

400 g (13 oz) **can condensed milk**

2 **bananas**

1 tablespoon **lemon juice**

150 ml (¼ pint) **whipping cream**

25 g (1 oz) **chocolate shavings**

125 g (4 oz) **plain flour**

pinch of **salt**

2 tablespoons **sugar**

1 **egg**, lightly beaten

300 ml (½ pint) **milk**

25 g (1 oz) **butter**, melted

vegetable oil or butter for greasing the pan

5

15

sweet pancakes

Add any topping you like – sugar and a squeeze of lemon, jam, chocolate sauce, or your favourite liqueur.

MAKES

8

easy

cheap

mates

1 Put the flour, salt and sugar into a bowl and make a hole in the centre. Pour the egg and a little of the milk into the hole. Whisk, slowly adding all the milk and melted butter to make a smooth paste. Pour into a jug or pint glass.

2 Put a little oil or butter into a frying pan and heat until it starts to smoke. Pour off any extra oil and pour a little batter into the pan, tilting the pan until the base is coated in a thin layer. Cook for 1–2 minutes until the bottom goes golden.

3 Flip the pancake over and cook for another 30–45 seconds until golden on the second side. Make the rest of the pancakes in the same way, greasing the pan if the pancakes start sticking.

mini raspberry pancakes

Great for a pudding or mid-afternoon snack. These cheeky little pancakes can be covered in any kind of jam or even chocolate sauce, depending on what you fancy.

1 Put the flour, sugar, baking powder, vanilla essence and eggs into a bowl. Slowly stir all the milk in, a little at a time, to make a smooth mixture.

2 Drop a little oil into a large frying pan. Heat for 1–2 minutes, then add a few large spoonfuls of the pancake mix to the pan, leaving space between each spoonful so that they don't all join up to make one big pancake!

3 Fry the pancakes for about 1 minute on the first side or until bubbles appear on the top of each pancake. Flip over and fry on the other side for about 1 minute until golden.

4 Put the cooked pancakes onto a plate, and carry on making pancakes until all the mixture is used up.

5 Spread the pancakes with butter, drizzle with maple syrup and sprinkle with raspberries. Roll them up if you fancy, then tuck in.

PREP

10

COOK

15

SERVES

2

fresh

posh

snack

200 g (7 oz) **self-raising flour**

25 g (1 oz) **sugar**

1 teaspoon **baking powder**

1 teaspoon **vanilla essence**

2 **eggs**

250 ml (8 fl oz) **milk**

vegetable oil, for greasing

butter, for spreading

maple syrup, to serve

125 g (4 oz) **raspberries** (defrosted, if frozen)

50 g (2 oz) **ground hazelnuts or almonds**, toasted

1 teaspoon **almond essence**

4 tablespoons **milk**

1 quantity **Sweet Pancake batter** (see page 190)

vegetable oil or butter, for frying

300 g (10 oz) **chocolate and hazelnut spread**

4 tablespoons **double cream**

5 large **bananas**

2 tablespoons **lemon juice**

icing sugar, for sprinkling

25 g (1 oz) **hazelnuts**, toasted and roughly chopped

PREP

25

COOK

25

SERVES

6

posh

party

sexy

chocolate and banana pancake torte

A fancy way to use pancakes – this is a really rich pudding, but not too filling.

1 Beat the ground nuts, almond essence and milk into the pancake batter and cook the pancakes following the Sweet Pancakes recipe (see page 190). Put the pancakes on a plate and make the filling.

2 Put the chocolate spread and cream in a small saucepan and heat over a low heat until slightly soft but not liquid.

3 Slice the bananas as thinly as you can and toss in the lemon juice.

4 Put a pancake on a plate and spread a little of the chocolate on top. Cover with a thin layer of banana slices, then put another pancake on top. Continue layering in this way, finishing up with a pancake. Sprinkle with icing sugar, scatter with toasted hazelnuts, cut into wedges and eat them with cream or ice cream.

fresh fruit salad

PREP

45*

COOK

SERVES

10

This delicious fruit combo is given extra sparkle by adding honey, wine and herbs. Ideal for a large party, you can use whatever fruit you like.

150 ml (¼ pint) **unsweetened pineapple juice**, chilled

125 g (4 oz) **honey**

250 g (8 oz) **canned lychees**

1 large **pineapple**, skinned, cored and diced or 1 400 g (13 oz) **can pineapple chunks**, drained

1 Mix together the pineapple juice and honey in a large bowl. When the honey has dissolved, tip in the lychees with their syrup. Add the pineapple, cherries, kiwi fruit and grapes. Put in the fridge for 4 hours, or overnight, if possible.

250 g (8 oz) **fresh or drained canned cherries**, pitted

4 **kiwi fruit**, peeled and thinly sliced

250 g (8 oz) **seedless black grapes**

2 Mix together the lemon juice and white wine. Then half an hour before you want to eat, stir the apples and bananas into the lemon juice mixture before stirring into the fruit salad. Pop back into the fridge for 30 minutes then dish up.

fast

75 ml (2 fl oz) **lemon juice**

125 ml (4 fl oz) **sweet white wine**

500 g (1 lb) **red dessert apples**, thinly sliced

3 large **bananas**, sliced

*Plus at least 4½ hours marinating and chilling

fruity

fresh

8 **bananas**, peeled

2 tablespoons **lemon juice**

8 tablespoons **brown sugar**

50 g (2 oz) **butter**

1 teaspoon **cinnamon**

Rum mascarpone cream:

250 g (8 oz) **mascarpone cheese**

2 tablespoons **rum**

1–2 tablespoons **sugar**

yum!

spicy

fruity

spiced bananas

Best cooked on the barbecue, these also make a tasty, warming snack when grilled – especially with a shot of the left-over rum!

1 Put each banana on a double piece of foil. Drizzle over the lemon juice and sprinkle 1 tablespoon of sugar on each.

2 Mix together the butter and cinnamon until creamy then dollop over the bananas.

3 Wrap each banana tightly in the foil and cook on the barbecue or under a medium grill for 10 minutes.

4 Meanwhile, make the rum mascarpone cream. Mix the cheese, rum and sugar together.

5 Unwrap the bananas and eat immediately with a dollop of the rum mascarpone cream.

fruit fritters with ice cream

Choose ripe but firm fruits for this pudding, such as peaches, apricots and nectarines, or even apples or bananas.

1 Mix the flour with a pinch of mixed spice and salt in a bowl. Beat in the egg yolk, melted butter and sparkling water to make a smooth batter.

2 Whisk the egg white in another bowl then slowly mix into the batter.

3 Heat 2.5 cm (1 inch) of oil in a deep saucepan.

4 Meanwhile, peel, pit, quarter or slice the fruit.

5 Dip the fruit into the batter and deep-fry for 1–2 minutes, until crisp and golden. Drain on kitchen paper.

6 Sprinkle the fritters with a little sugar and eat with ice cream.

PREP

15

COOK

10

SERVES

2

cool

fast

mates

40 g (1½ oz) **plain flour**

pinch of **ground mixed spice**

salt

1 **egg**, separated

15 g (½ oz) **butter**, melted

75 ml (3 fl oz) **sparkling water**

125 g (4 oz) **fresh fruit**

vegetable oil, for deep-frying

sugar, to sprinkle

ice cream, to serve

6 **gingernut biscuits**, roughly crushed

200 g (7 oz) **cream cheese**

200 g (7 oz) **fromage frais**

few drops of **vanilla essence**

1 tablespoon **sugar**

grated rind and juice of 1 **lime**

125 g (4 oz) **raspberries**

PREP

30

COOK

MAKES

4

easy

fruity

fresh

individual lime and raspberry cheesecakes

These are unbelievably quick and simple to make. A crunchy base topped with a creamy, fresh-tasting citrus filling and juicy berries – a perfect summer pudding.

1 Divide the biscuits between 4 small dishes or glasses.

2 In a bowl, mix together the cream cheese, fromage frais, vanilla essence, sugar, and lime rind and juice.

3 Spoon the mix onto the biscuits, then top with the raspberries and eat straight away.

grilled tropical fruits

PREP

COOK

SERVES

Fragrant, juicy tropical fruits make this speedy pudding rather exotic, but almost any fruit can be used.

1 large **mango**

1 **papaya**

1 small **pineapple,** or 1 400 g (13 oz) **can pineapple chunks,** drained

2 **kiwi fruit**

25 g (1 oz) **butter**, melted

1 piece **preserved stem ginger**, plus 2 tablespoons **syrup from the jar**

2 **passion fruit**

1 Cut the mango lengthways, either side of the stone, then cut the flesh from the skin and cut into chunks.

2 Halve the papaya, scoop out the seeds, then peel and cut the flesh into wedges.

3 Cut the skin off the pineapple, then quarter the pineapple lengthways and cut out the core. Cut into wedges.

4 Peel and quarter the kiwi fruit.

posh

5 Line a grill pan with foil, bringing the foil up over the sides of the pan to keep in the juices. Put a single layer of fruit in the pan. Brush with the butter and spoon over the ginger syrup.

6 Thinly slice the stem ginger, then cut each slice into even thin bits. Scatter over the fruits and grill in batches for about 5 minutes until the fruits are starting to colour. Put in bowls, pouring any juices from the pan over the top.

juicy

7 Halve the passion fruit, scoop out the middle, and spoon over each bowl of fruit salad.

fast

25 g (1 oz) **butter**, plus extra for greasing

50 g (2 oz) **brown sugar**

250 g (8 oz) **can pineapple rings**, drained

4 **glacé cherries**, cut in half

Sponge:

125 g (4 oz) **butter**, softened

125 g (4 oz) **sugar**

2 **eggs**, lightly beaten

½ teaspoon **mixed spice**

175 g (6 oz) **self-raising flour**

PREP

15

COOK

50

SERVES

4

fruity

cool

fab

pineapple upside-down pudding

You can use other canned fruits like apricot halves, peach halves or slices, or pear halves – it just depends what you like and what you have in your cupboard.

1 Heat the oven to 180°C (350°F), Gas Mark 4.

2 Lightly grease a 15 cm (6 inch) round cake tin or similar. Melt the butter in a saucepan, add the sugar and pour over the base of the tin. Put the pineapple rings and cherries in the base, the cherries rounded side facing down.

3 To make the sponge, mix the butter and sugar until soft and creamy. Slowly beat in the eggs then stir in the spice and flour. Pour over the fruit, smooth the top and bake in the oven for about 50 minutes or until the sponge is firm and golden.

4 Turn the sponge upside-down onto a plate, then dish up with custard or ice cream.

lime meringue pie

Beautifully light crispy meringue over a tangy lime filling – a real treat!

1 Heat the oven to 220°C (425°F), Gas Mark 7.

2 Lay the pastry over the inside of a greased 23 cm (9 inch) or similar ovenproof dish. Push gently into place and prick the base with a fork. Cover with a piece of greaseproof paper and fill the bottom with a layer of cheap dried beans. Bake for 10 minutes.

3 Remove the paper and beans and bake for another 10–12 minutes until crisp. Take out of the oven and turn the temperature down to 190°C (375°F), Gas Mark 5.

4 Make the filling: put the grated lime rind and juice in a saucepan with the sugar and eggs. Cook over a very low heat and stir well. Add the butter, one cube at a time, stirring all the time, until the mixture is hot.

5 Pour the lime mix into the pastry case and bake in the oven for about 10 minutes. Take out of the oven then leave to cool.

6 Beat the egg whites until they stand up in stiff peaks. Beat in the sugar a little at a time. Pile the meringue on top of the pie and bake for 12–15 minutes, until lightly brown.

PREP

15

COOK

50

SERVES

6

posh

party

saucy

450 g (15½ oz) pack **ready-rolled shortcrust pastry**, defrosted if frozen

Filling:

grated rind and juice of 3 **limes**

175 g (6 oz) **caster sugar**

3 **eggs**, beaten

250 g (8 oz) **butter**, cut into cubes

Meringue:

3 **egg whites**

75 g (3 oz) **caster sugar**

8 **sponge fingers or** 100 g (3½ oz) **plain sponge or jam Swiss roll**

3 tablespoons **orange juice**

375 g (12 oz) **frozen mixed summer fruits**, just defrosted

425 g (14 oz) ready-made **custard**

3 **egg whites**

75 g (3 oz) **sugar**

fruity

yum!

boozy

warm summer fruit trifle

Trifle's always popular – and if you want to liven it up just add a bit of sherry or sweet white wine with the orange juice.

1 Heat the oven to 160°C (325°F), Gas Mark 3.

2 Crumble the sponge into the base of an ovenproof dish. Drizzle the orange juice over the top then add the mixed fruits. Dollop the custard over the top.

3 Whisk the egg whites until really stiff, then whisk in the sugar, a spoonful at a time. Whisk for a minute or two more once all the sugar has been added until the mixture looks smooth and glossy.

4 Spoon the egg mix over the top of the custard in large swirls. Cook in the oven for 20 minutes until the meringue is golden brown on top, then eat while warm.

summer pudding

This most traditional of puddings has such a delicious colour. All you need is a glass of rosé wine to make a great summer treat.

1 Cut the crusts off the bread and line the base and sides of a pudding basin, fitting the bread pieces closely and cutting any excess away. Keep enough bread to make the top.

2 Put any currants you are using in a pan with the sugar and water. Heat gently until the sugar melts.

3 Take off the heat, add the liqueur and the rest of the fruit. Push the fruit through a sieve, keeping the juice. Spoon the fruit into the dish with half the juice and cover with the rest of the bread.

4 Cover with clingfilm then weigh down with a weighted plate and put in the fridge overnight. Put the juice in the fridge as well.

5 Take the plate off the pudding and run a knife around it. Put the basin on a plate and tip upside-down and gently shake so the pudding comes out. Pour over the rest of the juice, scatter some fresh fruit on top, and dish up with yogurt or fromage frais.

*Plus overnight chilling

PREP

30*

COOK

15

SERVES

6

posh

cool

juicy

300 g (10 oz) **white bread**

875 g (1¾ lb) **mixed summer fruits**, such as redcurrants, blackcurrants, raspberries, strawberries and cherries

75 g (3 oz) **sugar**

75 ml (3 fl oz) **water**

a little **liqueur**, such as framboise, crème de cassis or kirsch

extra fruit, to top

40 g (1½ oz) **butter**

4 slices white **bread**, crusts removed

4 tablespoons **apricot jam**

25 g (1 oz) **mixed peel**

25 g (1 oz) **sultanas**

450 ml (¾ pint) **milk**

2 tablespoons **sugar**

2 **eggs**, beaten

1 tablespoon **sherry**

PREP

10*

COOK

60

SERVES

4

easy

mates

cheap

bread and butter pudding

A real school-dinner pudding – but at least now you can add a glug of sherry to it if you like.

1 Grease a 1.2 litre (2 pint) or similar oven-proof dish with 15 g (½ oz) of the butter.

2 Butter the bread and spread with the apricot jam. Cut the slices into small triangles, then layer in the dish, sprinkling the mixed peel and sultanas between the layers.

3 Put the milk and sugar into a saucepan and heat until nearly boiling. Take off the heat and whisk in the eggs then the sherry. Pour over the bread and leave to soak for 30 minutes.

4 Meanwhile, heat the oven to 180°C (350°F), Gas Mark 4.

5 Put the dish into a roasting tin and fill with water to halfway up the sides. Bake in the oven for 45 minutes. Turn up the heat to 190°C (375°F), Gas Mark 5 and cook for another 10–15 minutes until crisp and golden on top, then dish up with custard.

*Plus 30 minutes soaking

gooey chocolate pudding

Sticky sponge with decadent chocolate sauce hidden underneath – what a sexy pudding.

1 Heat the oven to 180°C (350°F), Gas Mark 4.

2 To make the sauce, put the cocoa and sugar in a bowl and slowly mix in the boiling water until smooth.

3 To make the pudding, put all the ingredients into a bowl and beat together until smooth.

4 Spoon the pudding mix evenly into a greased ovenproof dish, then pour the sauce over the top. Bake in the oven for 15 minutes until the sauce has sunk to the bottom and the pudding has risen. Eat hot with vanilla ice cream.

yum!

gooey

share

Sauce:

2 tablespoons **cocoa powder**

50 g (2 oz) **brown sugar**

250 ml (8 fl oz) boiling **water**

Pudding:

75 g (3 oz) soft **margarine or butter**, softened, plus extra for greasing

75 g (3 oz) **brown sugar**

65 g (2½ oz) **self-raising flour**

3 tablespoons **cocoa powder**

3 **eggs**

½ teaspoon **baking powder**

4 **eggs**, separated

125 g (4 oz) **sugar**

125 g (4 oz) **chocolate**, broken into pieces

3 tablespoons **water**

300 ml (½ pint) **double cream**

To top:

25 ml (1 fl oz) **whipping cream**

25 g (1 oz) **chocolate shavings**

PREP

COOK

SERVES

sexy

yum!

easy

chocolate mousse

Top tip – to make a really light and fluffy chocolate pudding whisk the egg whites at room temperature.

1 Put the egg yolks and sugar into a bowl and whisk until thick.

2 Melt the chocolate with the water in a heat-proof bowl set over a saucepan of simmering water or melt in the microwave. Take off the heat and leave to cool slightly, then whisk into the egg yolk mix.

3 Whip the cream until firm, then mix slowly into the chocolate.

4 Whisk the egg whites until stiff, then mix 1 tablespoon into the mousse, before slowly mixing in the rest. Pour into 4–6 cups and put in the fridge to set.

5 Whip the whipping cream, put a dollop onto each mousse and then sprinkle with chocolate curls before eating. Looks great!

*Plus setting time

victoria sandwich cake

With the wonderful smell of baking filling your kitchen, you will be hard-pressed to resist eating this cake until it cools.

PREP

15

COOK

25

MAKES

1

posh

party

fab

125 g (4 oz) **butter or margarine**, plus extra for greasing

125 g (4 oz) **caster sugar**

2 **eggs**

125 g (4 oz) **self-raising flour**

1 tablespoon hot **water**

To fill and top:

3 tablespoons **jam**

150 ml (¼ pint) **double cream**, lightly whipped

icing sugar

1 Line and grease two 18 cm (7 inch) cake tins. Heat the oven to 180°C (350°F), Gas Mark 4.

2 Mix together the butter or margarine and sugar until light and fluffy. Beat in the eggs, one at a time, adding a tablespoon of the flour with the second egg. Fold in the rest of the flour, then the water.

3 Split the mixture between the two tins and bake in the oven for 20–25 minutes, until the cakes are golden and springy. Turn out onto a wire rack or plate and leave to cool.

4 Spread the jam on the top of one cake, followed by the whipped cream. Put the second cake on top of the first and sprinkle icing sugar over it all. Lovely!

carrot cakes

175 g (6 oz) **self-raising flour**

125 g (4 oz) **brown sugar**

2 teaspoons **baking powder**

1 teaspoon **ground cinnamon**

pinch of **ground nutmeg**

3 **eggs**, beaten

150 ml (¼ pint) **vegetable oil**, plus extra for greasing

1 teaspoon **vanilla essence**

250 g (8 oz) **carrots**, grated

Icing:

75 g (3 oz) **cream cheese**

1 teaspoon **vanilla essence**

50 g (2 oz) **icing sugar**

PREP

COOK

MAKES

easy

fun

yum!

Carrot cake not only tastes great, but is bursting with goodness and vitamins.

1 Heat the oven to 180°C (350°F), Gas Mark 4.

2 Put the flour, sugar, baking powder, cinnamon and nutmeg in a bowl, stir well, then make a hole in the centre. Mix in the eggs, oil, vanilla and carrots.

3 Spoon the mix into 10 paper cases or greased cups in a muffin tray. Bake in the oven for 25–30 minutes, until risen and golden brown, then leave to cool on a wire rack or plate.

4 To make the icing, mix the cream cheese, vanilla and icing sugar together in a bowl until smooth.

5 Swirl a spoonful of icing on top of each cake once cool and enjoy.

banana muffins

PREP

20

COOK

20

MAKES

10

These are a surprisingly good hangover cure, as bananas are a great, slow-releasing energy source known to soothe dodgy stomachs.

1 Heat the oven to 190°C (375°F), Gas Mark 5.

2 Mix the flour, baking powder and cinnamon in a bowl. Stir in the nutmeg, almonds and sugar.

3 Mash the bananas and mix in the eggs, oil, milk and honey to make a sloppy paste, then add to the dry ingredients and mix well.

4 Spoon into 10 paper cases or greased cups in a muffin tray and bake in the oven for 20–25 minutes until well risen.

mates

fruity

snack

200 g (7 oz) **plain flour**

3 teaspoons **baking powder**

1½ teaspoons **ground cinnamon**

pinch of **ground nutmeg**

50 g (2 oz) **ground almonds**

50 g (2 oz) **sugar**

2–3 **bananas**

2 **eggs**

2 tablespoons **vegetable oil**, plus extra for greasing

125 ml (4 fl oz) **milk**

3 tablespoons **honey**

125 g (4 oz) **butter**, softened, plus extra for greasing

125 g (4 oz) **sugar**

2 **eggs**

100 g (4 oz) **self-raising flour**

½ teaspoon **baking powder**

1 teaspoon **vanilla essence**

50 g (2 oz) **desiccated coconut**

150 g (5 oz) **blueberries**

PREP

10

COOK

25

MAKES

10

fruity

cool

juicy

coconut and blueberry cakes

Moist, fruity and enticingly dotted with blueberries, these fairy cakes are a perfect treat.

1 Heat the oven to 180°C (350°F), Gas Mark 4.

2 Put the butter, sugar and eggs in a bowl and mix. Add the flour and baking powder and mix, then add the vanilla. Beat well until light and creamy. Stir in the coconut and blueberries then spoon into 10 paper cases or greased cups in a muffin tray.

3 Bake in the oven for 20–25 minutes until risen and firm, then take out of the oven and put on a wire rack or plate to cool – if you can resist them until then.

very chunky chocolate brownies

Chocolate brownies are an all-time favourite. Gooey, sugary and rich, you can't beat these for a chocolate fix.

PREP

COOK

MAKES

300 g (10 oz) **plain chocolate**, broken into pieces

225 g (7½ oz) **butter**, softened, plus extra for greasing

3 **eggs**

225 g (7½ oz) **sugar**

75 g (3 oz) **self-raising flour**

175 g (6 oz) **walnuts**, broken up

200 g (7 oz) **milk chocolate**, broken into pieces

1 Grease a 28 x 20 cm (11 x 8 inch) or similar shallow baking tin. Heat the oven to 190°C (375°F), Gas Mark 5.

2 Melt the plain chocolate either in a heatproof bowl set over a saucepan of simmering water or melt it in the microwave, then stir in the butter.

3 Beat the eggs and sugar, then mix in the chocolate and butter mixture. Stir in the flour, walnuts and milk chocolate.

4 Pour into the tin, level the surface, then bake in the oven for about 40 minutes until the crust feels firm but is soft underneath. Do not overcook the brownies as you want them gooey. Leave in the tin to cool, if you can wait that long, then cut into squares.

yum!

sexy

gooey

75 g (3 oz) **ready-to-eat dried prunes**

75 g (3 oz) **ready-to-eat dried apricots**

100 g (3½ oz) **butter**, plus extra for greasing

100 g (3½ oz) **sugar**

5 tablespoons **honey**

375 g (12 oz) **porridge oats**

75 g (3 oz) **raisins or sultanas**

2 **eggs**

PREP

COOK

MAKES

snack

fruity

fresh

really fruity flapjacks

Flapjacks are so quick and easy to make. You can also use chopped figs or dates, or for extra tang, just add the grated rind of 1 lemon at the same time as the melted butter.

1 Grease a 28 x 23 cm (11 x 9 inch) shallow baking tin, or similar. Heat the oven to 180°C (350°F), Gas Mark 4.

2 Chop the prunes and apricots into small pieces.

3 Melt the butter, sugar and honey in a saucepan. Take off the heat and mix in the oats, prunes, apricots and raisins or sultanas. Leave to cool for 5–10 minutes then beat in the eggs.

4 Pour the mixture into the tin and level out. Bake in the oven for 20 minutes until pale golden, but still soft. Leave in the tin until cool, then chop up and put on a plate until cold and crunchy.

chocolate biscuit cake

This fridge cake is so moreish so make sure you don't leave it lying around or your flat-mates will devour it instantly.

1 Grease an 18 cm (7 inch) round cake tin or similar. Melt the plain chocolate and milk, then stir in the butter. Leave the mixture until cool, but not solid.

2 Break the digestive biscuits into small pieces and mix with the white and milk chocolate buttons.

3 Stir the biscuit mix into the melted chocolate, then pour into the tin and squash it down gently. Put in the fridge for at least 3 hours until firm, then cut into wedges.

*Plus at least 3 hours cooling and chilling

PREP

15*

COOK

MAKES

1

sexy

yum!

party

300 g (10 oz) **plain chocolate**, broken into pieces

2 tablespoons **milk**

125 g (4 oz) **butter**, melted, plus extra for greasing

125 g (4 oz) **digestive biscuits**

2 packets **white chocolate buttons**

2 packets **milk chocolate buttons**

25 g (1 oz) **butter or margarine**, plus extra for greasing

25 g (1 oz) **brown sugar**

125 g (4 oz) **golden syrup**

1 tablespoon **molasses or black treacle**

175 g (6 oz) **flour**

2 teaspoons **ground ginger**

1 teaspoon **bicarbonate of soda**

2 **eggs**, beaten

5 fl oz (¼ pint) **hot water**

PREP

15

COOK

45

MAKES

15

fun

share

gooey

sticky gingerbread

A really crunchy biscuit that lasts well so you can make a big batch and have a tasty snack whenever you want one.

1 Grease a 28 x 23 cm (11 x 9 inch) baking tin. Heat the oven to 180°C (350°F), Gas Mark 4.

2 Melt the butter or margarine, sugar, golden syrup and molasses or treacle in a saucepan until the sugar has dissolved.

3 Mix the flour, ginger and bicarbonate of soda in a bowl. Pour the sugar mix into the bowl and mix well. Add the beaten eggs and hot water, and mix to make a smooth batter.

4 Pour the batter into the tin and bake for 45 minutes, until golden and springy, then put on a wire rack or plate to cool.

gingerbread people

Have fun making these yummy biscuits. You don't have to make the traditional people shapes if you don't want to – just use your imagination...

1 Grease a large baking tin. Heat the oven to 180°C (350°F), Gas Mark 4.

2 Mix the flour and ginger in a bowl.

3 In another bowl, mix the butter and sugar until light and fluffy, then add the flour, ginger and the molasses, mix, and knead until smooth.

4 Lightly flour a surface and roll out the dough to 1 cm (½ in) thick. Make into gingerbread men shapes, with raisins for eyes and buttons, and candied fruit peel for the mouth – or make whatever shapes you want.

5 Bake in the oven for 20 minutes, then cool on a wire rack or plate.

PREP

15

COOK

20

MAKES
6

mates

cool

keeps

175 g (6 oz) **plain flour**

1 teaspoon **ground ginger**

25 g (1 oz) **butter or margarine**, plus extra for greasing

25 g (1 oz) **brown sugar**

1 tablespoon **molasses or black treacle**

To top:

raisins

candied fruit peel

200 g (7 oz) **plain flour**

1 teaspoon **bicarbonate of soda**

125 g (4 oz) **sugar**

125 g (4 oz) **butter**, cut into cubes, plus extra for greasing

1 **egg**

1 tablespoon **milk**

150 g (5 oz) **white chocolate**

75 g (3 oz) **glacé cherries**

PREP

COOK

MAKES

18

share

easy

snack

chunky monkeys

The perfect thing to nibble on while watching a soppy movie with a cup of tea – plus the aroma of freshly cooked biscuits will make your house smell so enticing that your friends won't want to leave.

1 Heat the oven to 180°C (350°F), Gas Mark 4.

2 Put the flour, bicarbonate of soda and sugar into a bowl and mix. Add the butter and rub into the flour mixture with your fingers until it looks like breadcrumbs.

3 Beat together the egg and milk. Chop the chocolate and cherries into rough pieces and add to the egg. Then mix into the flour and stir well until smooth.

4 Drop heaped spoonfuls of the cookie mixture, well spaced apart, on to a greased baking sheet and bake in the oven for 8–12 minutes until slightly brown. Leave to harden for 2 minutes, then put on a wire rack or plate to cool.

chunky choc cookies

These are surprisingly healthy as the seeds and oats have loads of good oils and fibre in them. So you needn't feel too guilty when you scoff them all!

1 Heat the oven to 180°C (350°C), Gas Mark 4.

2 Mix together the oats, flour, sesame and sunflower seeds in a bowl.

3 Melt the butter and sugar in a saucepan. Add to the oats, flour and seeds then mix in the oil and egg until combined. Stir in the chocolate drops.

4 Put spoonfuls of the mixture on a greased baking tray, spacing them slightly apart and flattening them with the back of a spoon.

5 Bake in the oven for about 15 minutes until golden but still slightly soft. Leave them to cool on a wire rack or plate and they will crisp up.

PREP

10

COOK

15

MAKES

15

mates

keeps

sexy

125 g (4 oz) **oats**

125 g (4 oz) **plain flour**

3 tablespoons **sesame seeds**

3 tablespoons **sunflower seeds**

75 g (3 oz) **butter**, plus extra for greasing

100 g (3½ oz) **sugar**

4 tablespoons **vegetable oil**

1 **egg**, lightly beaten

75 g (3 oz) **plain or milk chocolate drops**

smooth movers

1 ripe **banana**

300 ml (½ pint) **milk**

1 tablespoon **smooth peanut butter**

PREP

5*

COOK

SERVES

2

fruity

cheap

yum!

banana and peanut butter smoothie

A fantastic start to the day as bananas are a great slow-releasing energy provider.

1 Peel and slice the banana and put in the freezer for at least 2 hours or overnight.

2 Blend the banana, milk and peanut butter until smooth, then pour into two glasses.

*Plus at least 2 hours freezing

Note
These smoothies can be made in a blender or food processor. If you haven't got one, find someone who has, as the results are well worth it!

peach and orange smoothie

This juicy, tasty smoothie has loads of Vitamin C, so is ideal to make when you are feeling a bit rundown.

1 Blend the peaches with the yogurt, orange juice and honey until smooth. Pour into two glasses, with a couple of ice cubes in each, and enjoy.

PREP

5

COOK

SERVES

2

easy

cool

fresh

400 g (13 oz) **can peaches** in juice, drained

150 g (5 oz) **peach or apricot yogurt**

200 ml (7 fl oz) **orange juice**

a little **honey**

4 large **apples**

250 g (8 oz) **blueberries**, fresh or frozen

5

2

easy

fresh

fun

apple and blueberry smoothie

If you can't get hold of blueberries then you can use raspberries, blackcurrants or strawberries instead.

1 Juice the apples, then blend with the blueberries and pour into two tumblers.

mango and pineapple smoothie

This deliciously exotic chilled smoothie is a real winner. The perfect way to cool down on a hot day.

1 Peel the mango and roughly chop the flesh then put in the freezer for at least 2 hours or overnight.

2 Blend the frozen mango with the pineapple juice, lime rind and juice until thick. Yum!

*Plus at least 2 hours freezing

PREP

5*

COOK

SERVES

2

1 ripe **mango**

300 ml (½ pint) **pineapple juice**

rind and juice of ½ **lime**

share

fruity

posh

¼ **watermelon**, about 300 g (10 oz) flesh

2 **kiwi fruit**

200 ml (7 fl oz) **passion fruit juice**

10*

2

cool

fruity

fast

kiwi, melon and passion fruit smoothie

The perfect pick-you-up. If you are feeling a bit under-the-weather then down one of these and wait for the vitamins to kick in.

1 Remove and throw out the seeds from the watermelon. Chop up the flesh then put in the freezer for at least 2 hours or overnight.

2 Peel and roughly chop the kiwi fruit and blend with the watermelon and passion fruit juice until thick.

*Plus at least 2 hours freezing

strawberry and pineapple smoothie

A great breakfast drink or a snack. If you want to boost the protein content then swap half the yogurt for tofu.

1 Roughly chop the strawberries and put in the freezer for at least 2 hours or overnight.

2 Blend the frozen strawberries, pineapple juice and yogurt until smooth. Pour into two glasses, add a couple of ice cubes to each, and top with strawberries.

*Plus at least 2 hours freezing

PREP

5*

COOK

SERVES

2

juicy

fresh

easy

150 g (5 oz) **strawberries**, hulled, plus extra to decorate

150 ml (¼ pint) **pineapple juice**

150 g (5 oz) **strawberry yogurt**

help for hangovers

100 g (3½ oz) **strawberries**, hulled

300 g (10 oz) **pineapple**, skinned, cored and diced, **or** 400 g (3 oz) **can pineapple**, drained

1 **banana**

ice cubes

PREP

5

acher shaker

COOK

If you ache from head to toe and can't seem to function, then you need this fruity smoothie to replace vital potassium, get some vitamin C into your system and give you some extra B vitamins.

SERVES

1

1 Juice the strawberries and pineapple, then blend with the banana and a couple of ice cubes and sip slowly.

fruity

fab

cool

Note
You'll need a proper juicer for these recipes, but it's an investment worth making. There are several different types so it's worth shopping around.

pick-me-up

Ginger helps to alleviate symptoms of nausea, and carrot and apple provide a welcome burst of nutrients.

1 Juice the carrots, apple and ginger. Pour the mixture into a glass and add a couple of ice cubes, then drink.

PREP

5

COOK

SERVES

1

easy

mates

fun

200 g (7 oz) **carrots**

1 tart apple, such as **Granny Smith**

1 cm (½ inch) piece of **fresh root ginger**, peeled and chopped

ice cubes

2 large **grapefruits**

1 **lemon**

1 **cucumber**

ice cubes

sparkling mineral water

To top:

chopped **mint**

cucumber slices

lemon slices

lemon aid

The cucumber will help to flush out your kidneys and the grapefruit will aid the elimination of toxins – both vital for hangover relief and recovery!

1 Peel the grapefruits and the lemon, leaving much of the pith on. Juice the grapefruit, cucumber and lemon. Pour into a jug filled with ice and top up with sparkling mineral water. Decorate with chopped mint and slices of cucumber and lemon and share with any other hangover sufferers.

fresh

juicy

easy

peach fizz

A great combo. Peach is soothing, while ginger works wonders for nausea.

1 Juice the peach and ginger and pour into a tall glass filled with ice. Add sparkling water to fill and a couple of mint leaves and sip slowly to calm your stomach.

PREP

5

COOK

SERVES

1

spicy

yum!

fab

250 g (8 oz) **peaches**

2.5 cm (1 inch) piece of **fresh root ginger**, peeled and roughly chopped

sparkling mineral water

mint leaves

500 g (1 lb) **cantaloupe melon**, peeled, or any melon flesh and seeds

ice cubes

5

morning glory

If you need to rehydrate, melon has a fantastically high water content and replenishes lost fluids very quickly, so you can get on with your day.

SERVES

1

1 Juice the melon, pour over ice and drink immediately.

cool

fruity

cheap

eye opener

Carrot and fennel are effective detoxifiers and good for restoring fluid balance. A glass of this juice should give you an immediate lift and ensure that the whites of your eyes are white, not bloodshot!

1 Juice the carrots and fennel. Pour into a tall glass filled with ice and drink.

PREP

5

COOK

SERVES

1

posh

fast

fab

200 g (7 oz) **carrots**

200 g (7 oz) **fennel**

ice cubes

100 g (3½ oz) **cauliflower**

200 g (7 oz) **carrots**

1 large **tomato**

ice cubes

10

COOK

SERVES

1

saucy

cheap

cool

veg out

If you want to thoroughly cleanse your kidneys and liver, then this juice is superb. Cauliflower helps to purify the blood and lower blood pressure, but it does have quite a strong taste. If you have a sweet tooth, add an apple to soften the flavour.

1 Juice the cauliflower, carrots and tomato. Pour over ice and drink.

the rehydrator

PREP

10

COOK

SERVES

1

1 **orange**

50 g (2 oz) **cucumber**

100 ml (3½ fl oz)
cranberry juice

ice cubes

If you are feeling really dehydrated, you are going to need more than just a glass of water to make you feel better! This juice, which is packed with Vitamin C, folic acid and potassium, will help replace some of the vital nutrients you lost the night before and quench that insatiable thirst.

1 Peel the orange, leaving on as much pith as possible. Juice the orange and cucumber. Mix the juice with the cranberry juice and pour into a tall glass over ice.

yum!

fresh

fab

1 large **pear**

100 ml (3½ fl oz) **cranberry juice**

ice cubes

COOK

SERVES

1

fast

fun

posh

hazy days

If your kidneys were aching when you woke up, then give them a good flush with this refreshing juice. The pectin in the pear will aid the removal of toxins, while cranberries are renowned for killing bacteria and viruses in the kidneys.

1 Juice the pear and mix the pear juice with the cranberry juice. Pour into a tall glass over ice and enjoy.

c double

2 large **oranges**

2 **kiwi fruit** (skins left on)

ice cubes

Remember that kiwi fruit contain even more vitamin C than oranges, so by combining the two fruits you are giving yourself a really potent dose. Just watch that hangover fade away.

1 Peel the oranges, leaving on as much pith as possible, and juice them along with the kiwi fruit. Then pour over ice and drink.

fruity

fab

juicy

125 g (4 oz) **papaya**

2 **oranges**

125 g (4 oz) **cucumber**

ice cubes

morning after

This fab juice will help to rehydrate you. Papaya helps to calm the digestive system, cucumber flushes out toxins and orange gives a great boost of vitamin C.

1 Peel the papaya and the oranges (leaving as much of the pith on as possible). Juice the papaya, oranges and cucumber and pour into a tall glass over ice.

cool

yum!

fresh

clear ahead

If you have woken up to find that your body has gone into toxic overload, then this is the ideal juice for you. Carrots contain huge amounts of vitamin A, and apples will help you to detox.

1 Juice the carrots, radishes and apple. Pour into a glass over the ice cubes and drink.

COOK

SERVES

1

fast

juicy

fun

250 g (8 oz) **carrots**

50 g (2 oz) **radishes**

1 large **apple**

ice cubes

the cocktail hour

manhattan

4–5 **ice cubes**

1 measure **sweet vermouth**

3 measures **whisky**

One of the best-known cocktails, this deserves to be a favourite.

1 Put the ice cubes into a glass. Pour the vermouth and whisky over the ice. Stir vigorously, then strain the liquid into a chilled cocktail glass.

daiquiri

3 **ice cubes**, cracked

juice of 2 **limes**

1 teaspoon **sugar syrup** (½ teaspoon of sugar and ½ teaspoon of boiling water)

3 measures **white rum**

A delightful mix of sweet and sour, where the limes and sugar syrup perfectly complement each other.

1 Put the cracked ice into a cocktail shaker or screw-top jar. Pour the lime juice, sugar syrup and rum over the ice. Shake thoroughly until you get a frosted effect, then strain into a chilled cocktail glass.

posh

piña colada

3 **ice cubes**, cracked

1 measure **white rum**

2 measures **coconut cream**

2 measures **pineapple juice**

cocktail cherry and **slice of orange**, to decorate

The ultimate in tacky drinks, as it needs a cocktail cherry and orange slice on the side of the glass. You really need to be wearing a Hawaiian shirt for this one!

1 Put the cracked ice, rum, coconut cream and pineapple juice into a cocktail shaker or screw-top jar. Shake lightly to mix. Strain into a large glass and decorate with the cherry and orange slice.

sea breeze

1 measure **vodka**

1½ measures **cranberry juice**

1½ measures **grapefruit juice**

5 **ice cubes**, cracked

For the true look decorate with a slice of lemon or lime and then drink with a straw.

1 Pour the vodka, cranberry juice and grapefruit juice into a tall glass with the ice cubes and mix well.

mates

6 **ice cubes**

1 measure **vodka**

125 ml (4 fl oz) **orange juice**

1–2 teaspoons **Galliano**

harvey wallbanger

The easiest way to 'float' the Galliano is to gently swirl the drink then pour the Galliano onto the back of a spoon, holding it just above the cocktail.

1 Put half the ice cubes, the vodka and orange juice into a cocktail shaker or screw-top jar. Shake well for about 30 seconds, then strain into a tall glass over the rest of the ice cubes. Float the Galliano on top.

2–3 **ice cubes**

1 measure **vodka**

2 measures **orange juice** or juice of 1 orange

screwdriver

Okay, so this is really just a vodka-and-orange, but sometimes the simple things are the best.

1 Put the ice cubes into a tall glass. Add the vodka and orange juice and stir lightly.

party

long island iced tea

A real classic, evoking thoughts of tropical islands and drinks on the verandah.

PREP

3

SERVES

1

6 **ice cubes**

½ measure **gin**

½ measure **vodka**

½ measure **white rum**

½ measure **tequila**

½ measure **Cointreau**

1 measure **lemon juice**

1 teaspoon **sugar syrup**
(⅛ teaspoon sugar and
½ teaspoon boiling water)

cola, to top up

slice of lemon

1 Put the ice cubes into a glass. Add the gin, vodka, rum, tequila, Cointreau, lemon juice and sugar syrup. Stir well, then strain into a tall glass almost filled with ice cubes. Top up with cola and chuck in a slice of lemon.

sex on the beach

For the full holiday effect you need to decorate the glass with a cherry and then drink with a straw.

PREP

3

SERVES

1

fab

⅛ measure **vodka**

½ measure **peach schnapps**

1 measure **cranberry juice**

1 measure **orange juice**

1 measure **pineapple juice**

3 **ice cubes**

1 Put the vodka, peach schnapps, cranberry juice, orange juice and pineapple juice into a cocktail shaker with the ice. Shake thoroughly then pour into a tall glass.

a little **lemon juice**

1 measure fresh **lime juice**, plus extra for rimming

salt

1½ measures **tequila**

1 measure **Cointreau**

2–3 **ice cubes**, cracked

slice of lime

margarita

A lethal concoction, and one that will certainly punish you if you drink too many!

1 Dip the rim of a chilled cocktail glass in lemon juice, then in the salt. Put the tequila, 1 measure of lime juice and Cointreau into a cocktail shaker or screw-top jar with the cracked ice. Shake thoroughly and strain into a cocktail glass with a salt rim. Decorate with a slice of lime.

2–3 **ice cubes**, cracked

1 measure **tequila**

½ measure **port**

1 teaspoon **lime juice**

2 dashes **Angostura bitters**

slice of lime

PREP

SERVES

tequila cocktail

This Mexican delight has been responsible for many a hangover.

1 Put the ice cubes into a cocktail shaker or screw-top jar. Add the tequila, port, lime juice and Angostura bitters and shake well. Strain into a cocktail glass and decorate with a slice of lime.

boozy

classic champagne

PREP

SERVES

A great way to start the evening – this cocktail will certainly liven you up and put you in the party mood.

1 **sugar lump**

1–2 dashes **Angostura bitters**

1 measure **brandy**

4 measures **champagne**, chilled

1 Put the sugar lump into a chilled cocktail or champagne glass and glug over the Angostura bitters. Add the brandy, then fill the glass with champagne.

buck's fizz

PREP

SERVES

An old favourite, and a good way to disguise cheap sparkling plonk.

1 measure **orange juice**, chilled

1 dash **grenadine**

2 measures **champagne**, chilled

1 Put the orange juice and grenadine in a wine glass or champagne glass and stir well. Top up with chilled champagne.

½ measure **Kahlúa**

½ measure **Bailey's Irish Cream**

½ measure **Grand Marnier**

b-52

A lovely creamy shooter, as all three luscious layers warm your throat on the way down.

1 Pour the Kahlúa into a shot glass. Using the back of a spoon, slowly pour the Bailey's to float over the Kahlúa. Pour the Grand Marnier over the Bailey's in the same way, and you will have a three-layered shooter.

4–5 **ice cubes**

¼ measure **dry vermouth**

3 measures **vodka**

1 **green olive**

PREP

2

SERVES

1

vodka martini

James Bond's choice of drink – he liked it shaken not stirred though.

1 Put the ice cubes into a glass. Pour the vermouth and vodka over the ice and stir vigorously, without splashing. Strain the mixture into a chilled cocktail glass, drop in the olive and drink.

cool

havana zombie

This tropical Cuban cocktail certainly has a kick, which isn't surprising as it uses three different kinds of rum.

1 Put the ice cubes into a glass. Pour the lime juice and pineapple juice, sugar syrup and rums over the ice and stir vigorously. Pour into a tall glass.

4–5 **ice cubes**

juice of **1 lime**

5 tablespoons **pineapple juice**

1 teaspoon **sugar syrup** (½ teaspoon sugar and ⅓ teaspoon boiling water)

1 measure **white rum**

1 measure **golden rum**

1 measure **dark rum**

hawaiian vodka

A fresh and fruity cocktail with a bit of a bite.

1 Put the ice cubes into a cocktail shaker or screw-top jar. Pour the pineapple, lemon and orange juices, grenadine and vodka over the ice and shake until a frost forms. Strain into a glass and decorate with a slice of lemon.

share

4–5 **ice cubes**

1 measure **pineapple juice**

juice of 1 **lemon**

juice of 1 **orange**

1 teaspoon **grenadine**

3 measures **vodka**

slice of lemon

sangria

20–30 **ice cubes**

2 bottles light Spanish **red wine**, chilled

125 ml (4 fl oz) **brandy**

450 ml (¾ pint) **soda water**, chilled

slices of **fruit**, such as apples, pears, oranges, lemons, peaches and strawberries

slices of orange

SERVES

A classic Spanish drink, this is a great cocktail for a party as long as you don't care about the carpets!

1 Put the ice into a large bowl and pour over the wine and brandy, if you have it. Give it a stir. Add soda water and chuck in a load of fruit on top. Put an orange slice on the side of each glass and pour in the Sangria.

PREP

havana beach

juice of ½ a **lime**

2 measures **pineapple juice**

1 measure **white rum**

1 teaspoon **sugar**

3–4 **ice cubes**

ginger ale, to top up

slice of lime

SERVES

A tasty, fruity drink. Just decorate with a slice of lime and drink with a straw and pretend you are on a white sandy beach.

1 Mix the lime juice, pineapple juice, rum and sugar until smooth. Put the ice into a tall glass, pour the drink on top and top up with ginger ale.

fresh

mai tai

One to go over the top with – decorate with cherries, pineapple and a slice of orange.

PREP

3

SERVES

1

egg white, lightly beaten

caster sugar, for frosting

1 measure **white rum**

½ measure fresh **orange juice**

½ measure fresh **lime juice**

3 crushed **ice cubes**

1 Dip the rim of a tall glass into the beaten egg white, then into the caster sugar. Put the rum, orange juice and lime juice into a cocktail shaker or screw-top jar and shake to mix. Put the ice into the glass and carefully pour the cocktail over it.

zombie

For the authentic Zombie spear a cherry and pineapple onto a cocktail stick and place it across the top of the glass before you drink it.

PREP

2

SERVES

1

sexy

3 **ice cubes,** cracked

1 measure **dark rum**

1 measure **white rum**

½ measure **apricot brandy**

2 measures **pineapple juice**

1 tablespoon **lime juice**

2 teaspoons **caster sugar**

1 Put the ice into a cocktail shaker or screw-top jar, add the rums, apricot brandy, fruit juices and sugar. Shake until a frost forms. Pour the drink into a tall, frozen glass.

tom collins

PREP

SERVES

ice cubes

juice of ½ a **lemon**

1½ teaspoons **caster sugar**

60 ml (2 fl oz) **gin**

soda water, to top up

Decorate with a slice of lemon and a cherry or try adding soda water to this cocktail to make a Gin Fizz.

1 Half-fill a cocktail shaker or screw-top jar with ice. Add the lemon juice, and stir in the sugar. Pour in the gin and shake well for 60 seconds. Strain into a tall glass, add more ice and top up with the soda water.

cosmopolitan

PREP

SERVES

6 **ice cubes**, cracked

1 measure **vodka**

½ measure **Cointreau**

1 measure **cranberry juice**

juice of ½ a **lime**

slice of lime

You can pretend this is doing you good as cranberry juice is great for your kidneys, and lime has loads of Vitamin C.

1 Put the ice in a cocktail shaker or screw-top jar and add the vodka, Cointreau, cranberry juice and lime juice. Shake until a frost forms. Strain into a cocktail glass and decorate with a slice of lime.

fun

sloe comfortable screw

PREP

3

A really good cocktail, with a fab mix of strong tastes. See if you can handle this one...

SERVES

1

6–8 **ice cubes**

½ measure **sloe gin**

½ measure **Southern Comfort**

1 measure **vodka**

2½ measures **orange juice**

1 Half-fill a tall glass with ice cubes. Pour the sloe gin, Southern Comfort, vodka and orange juice into the glass and stir well.

kamikaze

PREP

2

Short and sweet. A great taste and a big kick.

SERVES

1

6 **ice cubes**, cracked

½ measure **vodka**

½ measure **Curaçao**

½ measure **lime juice**

1 Put the ice in a cocktail shaker or screw-top jar and add the vodka, Curaçao and lime juice. Shake until a frost forms, then strain into a shot glass.

mates

index

a

anchovies, bruschetta with
    tomatoes and 63
apples: apple and blueberry
    smoothie 220
    fruit crumble 186
aubergines: lentil, aubergine and
    coconut dhal 183
    moussaka 141
    tofu ragout 108
    vegetable moussaka 114
avocados: avocado sauce 127
    guacamole 77
    spinach, avocado and bacon
        salad 74

b

B-52 246
bacon: club sandwich 57
    croque madame 59
    pasta with tomato and bacon
        sauce 31
    potato and bacon gratin 32
    quick pasta carbonara 89
    tagliatelle with mushrooms
        and 160
baked beans: baked bean
        cassoulet 157
    cottage pie 29
    spicy tortillas 158
balti chicken 172
bananas: banana and peanut
        butter smoothie 218
    banana muffins 207
    banoffi pie 189
    chocolate and banana pancake
        torte 192
    spiced bananas 194

barbecued ribs 91
beans: chicken enchiladas 134
    chilli bean and carrot soup 53
    chilli bean bake 113
    chilli con carne 27
    easy bean and pepper bake 112
    veggie burgers 118
    veggie sausages and beans 117
    see also baked beans
beef: beef stroganoff 139
    beer-braised beef 144
    chilli con carne 27
    great steak sandwich 85
    Italian meatballs 142
    lasagne 137
    moussaka 141
    roast beef 164
    spaghetti bolognese 136
    spicy beefburgers 28
    spicy tortillas 158
    stir-fried beef with baby
        sweetcorn 175
    Thai beef and mixed pepper
        stir-fry 176
biscuits: chunky choc
        cookies 215
    chunky monkeys 214
    gingerbread people 213
black bean sauce, fish with 150
blueberries: coconut and blueberry
        cakes 208
    Italian trifle 187
Bolognese sauce 98, 136
bread: bread and butter
        pudding 202
    bruschetta 63, 123
    eggy bread 20
    garlic bread 62
    sandwiches 57–61, 85
    summer pudding 201
    tasty open toasties 56
breakfast gratin 81

broad beans: falafel 119
    spicy meat and bean pasta 143
broccoli and chicken risotto 133
bruschetta 63, 123
buck's fizz 245
burgers, veggie 118
burritos with pork stuffing 146

c

cabbage: spicy coleslaw 76
Caesar salad 73
cakes: carrot cakes 206
    chocolate biscuit cake 211
    coconut and blueberry cakes 208
    sticky gingerbread 212
    very chunky chocolate
        brownies 209
    Victoria sandwich cake 205
cannelloni: chicken 138
    spinach 100
carrots: carrot cakes 206
    chilli bean and carrot soup 53
    chunky carrot and lentil soup 48
    clear ahead 237
    eye opener 231
    pick-me-up 227
    veg out 232
casseroles 25, 144–5, 148, 157
cauliflower cheese 121
champagne cocktails 245
cheat's calzone 90
cheese: cauliflower cheese 121
    cheat's calzone 90
    cheesy spinach lasagne 99
    classic tomato pizza 43
    croque madame 59
    croque monsieur 58
    dinner jackets 26
    dumplings 144
    French toast sandwiches 60
    ham and cheese pancakes 37
    lasagne 137

Acknowledgements
Executive Editor Nicky Hill
Editor Rachel Lawrence
Book Design Rozelle Bentheim
Designer Miranda Harvey
Production Controller Jo Sim

With special thanks to
David Preston for his work
on the typography.